T0196987

*Spirit of a*
# SOUND MIND

## CATHERINE E. GOIN

WESTBOW
PRESS®
A DIVISION OF THOMAS NELSON
& ZONDERVAN

WestBow Press books may be ordered through booksellers or by contacting:

WestBow Press
A Division of Thomas Nelson & Zondervan
1663 Liberty Drive
Bloomington, IN 47403
www.westbowpress.com
844-714-3454

Because of the dynamic nature of the Internet, any web addresses or links contained in this book may have changed since publication and may no longer be valid. The views expressed in this work are solely those of the author and do not necessarily reflect the views of the publisher, and the publisher hereby disclaims any responsibility for them.

Any people depicted in stock imagery provided by Getty Images are models, and such images are being used for illustrative purposes only. Certain stock imagery © Getty Images.

Scripture taken from the New King James Version®. Copyright © 1982 by Thomas Nelson. Used by permission. All rights reserved.

ISBN: 978-1-6642-5921-8 (sc)
ISBN: 978-1-6642-5922-5 (hc)
ISBN: 978-1-6642-5920-1 (e)

Library of Congress Control Number: 2022903713

Print information available on the last page.

WestBow Press rev. date: 05/13/2022

*Other books by Catherine E. Goin:*

**Mercy Lord, Mercy**
**A Broken-hearted Schizophrenic**

Dedicated to my immediate family----Russell Goin, Catherine and Howard Goin

Thanks to: Dr. Stanley Wang, Dr. Zigmund Lebensohn, Dr. David Goldstein, Dr. Schwartz and Dr. Myron Wentz

Chance! Oh, there is no chance! The scene
Is set.
Up with the curtain! Man, the marionette,
Resumes his part. The gods will work the
wires.
They've got it all down fine, you bet, you bet!

From "Quatrains" in "The Spell of the
Yukon" by Robert Service

**Dear Reader:**

**The Stars were Lost**

It all began on a cloudy Easter morning in 1974. The constant drone of my schizophrenic voices were telling me I needed to do something bad. They told me I wanted to defy God. Deep inside, I wanted God to punish me, to have Him end my life. It all sounded terrific, perhaps meaningful.

The next steps felt effortless. I found an old Bible in my apartment, placed it in the Japanese iron cooking pot I used to stir-fry and as the fog horns called out across the city, I lit a match to the pages. Nothing happened but smoke and fire. No lightning bolts... no deep thundering voice screaming out my damnation... just billowing plumes filling the kitchen all the way to the ceiling. My eyes watered. Thumbing my nose at God hadn't worked so I left my apartment and went for a walk as the fog drifted across the Marina.

Over a period of a few troubled weeks of walking I considered the possibilities. Maybe God was dead? Maybe God wasn't vengeful? Maybe the world had gone mad? Or maybe it was me? I walked the streets, ate very little, and couldn't sleep.

On May 14th, 1974 I called the police department and told them that help was needed immediately. They gave me the address of a drug rehab clinic several miles away. It was late at night. I started walking. The space ships were after me. I sensed their wires inside my brain, a hum of voices. The stars were out of place and lost. By the time I reached the clinic it had occurred to me my problem wasn't drugs. It was something more horrible and profound.

Across from the clinic there was a service station where I sat on a pile of old tires which provided me a place to think. From the phone booth I once again called the police. "It isn't drugs," I said. "I either belong in jail or the hospital." The police arrived quickly in their gaily painted car. I walked to their car, pulled out my leopard printed pocket knife and offered it to them. After a quick drive, they checked me out at the police station and then drove on to a health clinic. At the clinic, I took Edgar Rice Burrough's "Princess of Mars" from my shoulder bag and began to quietly and calmly read. Soon, the clinic staff was by my side, ready to ask questions. "The stars are out of place," I said. And then the flood gates broke... screaming was uncontrollable. Fear and the possibility of relief surged inside me. The ambulance arrived and a straight jacket was placed on me. I thought that rather odd but the orderly said "Just consider it a seat belt." Around midnight on May 14, 1974 I found myself on the sixteenth floor of St. Francis Hospital sick and horribly nervous.

# Contents

# The Psychiatric Ward

You never know who you're going to meet in a psychiatric ward. It was San Francisco. My doctor was a Chinese Southern Baptist psychiatrist who told me to stop screaming and gave me a shot in the arm. "What's wrong young lady," he asked in a kind voice.

"'The stars are out of place'" I said. He assured me all would be much better tomorrow. I was out like a light.

The next morning, after I awoke with a cotton mouth, Dr. Wang stopped by on his rounds. He talked to me, listening attentively to my confused state. He must have seen how thin I was, thirty pounds less than a slim young woman should be. Within in few moments, he looked at me straight on and in a firm and calm voice said, "Miss Goin, you will eat or die."

Die! It had come to that. I hadn't eaten for days. My thinking was out of control. But eating? Food was my enemy, my nemesis, the cause of fatness, disfigurement, ugliness, and shame. But dying hadn't occurred to me and deep inside I no longer wanted to die.

"Your body is sacred and a temple of God, Miss Goin. You'll be in the hospital for tests and rest. And you'll eat. You have two weeks to get better and I promise you will."

Dr. Wang told me he'd be spending time with me almost every day. He promised no one would be coming to see me that I didn't want as a visitor. For the first time in years I felt safe. No one had ever seen me or spoken to me so clearly and without judgment.

Over the days we met, I recall his solid, unflappable presence. I felt the stars returning to their natural order and the universe more whole and balanced. In reflecting on this hospitalization, I was blessed to be in the kind and capable care of someone who saw in me something much more than the symptoms of my troubled world.

The next two weeks in the hospital offered a world apart. The bars on the windows, the locks on the doors, and a prominent security guard ensured that. The 30 or so men and women confined to the beige and dusty blue walls of the sixteenth floor were in a reality all their own.

Room after room merged into one large hall: rooms for sleeping with white covers and single metal beds, bathrooms with white sinks and shiny mirrors, private commodes and showers with curtains, a large dining room for eating and watching TV with rows of tables and chairs, and a small arts and crafts room with drawings of birds and trees on the walls. It was comfortable and a place of few distractions where I could keep to myself. During the mornings, I sat in the arts and crafts room shaping clay into science fiction characters. In the afternoon, I'd move to a large couch in the main hall making sketches of patients and plants with a ball point pen. The heavy medication kept me tired but calm.

# Madness Coming to a Head

**B**efore the hospital, I'd been living alone and not working for several months. For strange behavior, I'd been put on sick list, required to use my accumulated sick leave and to check with a doctor investigating to attempt to determine what was wrong. My supervisor suspected drug use. The doctors couldn't tell. By February, my roommate moved out, relieving me finally of his presence but isolating me inside my troubled mind.

The event leading up to my medical leave of absence occurred on a DC- 10. We had landed at the San Francisco airport and the on-ground agent was waiting for the passengers to disembark through the jet way. "Disarm my slide" a stewardess said. But something inside me said "No, go ahead, open the door first." So, I did. And within seconds yellow rubber and air shot out from the plane with a loud whoosh. The huge bright yellow slide covered the tarmack, the agent nearby barely escaping the forceful explosion. I was shocked. A tense silence filled the plane. A supervisor hurriedly pulled me aside. A wave of fear and confusion flooded my senses. My career as a Flight Attendant was over!... I thought.

The next day I was called to a special meeting. A gathering of managers sat at a large wooden table, looked at me sternly, and told me I couldn't fly. This time it was decided I had to take a medical leave of absence and had to go to the company's doctor to find out what was wrong, and if my problem wasn't successfully addressed, I'd be terminated. During the bus ride home, my mind focused on other things: beautiful shoes calling me from the fancy store windows and dark worn shoes staring up at me from the feet on that San Francisco bus. I walked the streets that night looking into the star-lit sky. Forlorn!

Within a few days, my appointment with the company doctor was set. We would meet three times in all. He was kind, thoughtful, and never condescending. "Was it drugs?" he asked. The way he looked at me showed he found it hard to believe me when I told him it wasn't. The frustration at my helplessness to know what was wrong with me was enormous. I was alone, not able to work, and trapped in a mind I could no longer rely upon. What had happened? Where could I find some help? I told the doctor I would find it on my own and tearfully stormed out of his office.

# Spaceship Floor 16

F orward to the hospital where I had been for a week when Mom and my younger brother Russell appeared. The company doctor and Dr. Wang had arranged for their visit. It was late spring. I'd been wearing the same clothes every day: blue jeans, a red and black lumberjack jacket, a tee shirt and heavy Frye boots. With unkempt hair and a pale and drawn face from the loss of 30 pounds, I must have looked to them like someone else. Without Mom's permission, I'd become unfamiliar and lost. There were no hugs or greetings. She handed me a pair of rose- colored trousers and a coordinated sweater. Pure ecstasy.

In thinking back, perhaps I'd suddenly become for her part of the family saga that had colored her entire adult life; a saga she had tried to bury and run from unsuccessfully. Was she imagining I'd become like my father's family; unreliable, and socially disgraced? The mask of superficial superiority I'd experienced throughout childhood was absent. In its place, there was something courageous about her; a quality of good sportsmanship coming to the surface even as she appeared embarrassed, afraid, stressed, even horrified.

Russell's reaction was entirely different. Without fanfare, expression, or underlying psychosis, the ultimate pragmatist called out across the table between us. "Betsy, if you don't get your act together, you're going to be in a crummy institution for the rest of your life."

That night, after Mom and Russel left, Dr. Wang introduced

me to the other patients in the large dining room. "The 16th floor is filled with people of all types. Right here in front of us there are drug addicts, alcoholics, manic depressives, schizophrenics, suicidally inclined, kleptomaniacs, people from the streets and good homes and they are all just like you." I took my seat among them in front of a large TV and as I watched my first episode of Star Trek, "The Trouble with Tribbles," I felt part of a new community. I felt happy to have found a comfortable spaceship that was safe and non-threatening. And with Mr. Spock I'd finally found a spiritual home, a role model and confidant that might help me get well. His ears and logic spoke to me. "Live long and prosper," he said.

Among those in the confines of the psychiatric ward, there were three patients I remember to this day. I referred to them as "Teddy", a very handsome alcoholic; "Princess Olga from Russia," an emaciated woman in her sixties who drifted throughout the ward chattering to herself, looking and acting very regal; and "Lucy", my roommate and the wife of a wealthy lawyer. She was being divorced by her husband because of her condition.

I may have remembered these people because they projected something about me. Teddy had the same disease my father had, and I loved drawing his handsome face. Princess Olga was amazingly thin as I'd once hoped to be and had found an ability to rise above the occasion of her illness. She also shared with me most of her food. Lucy, my roommate, was pretty and lost, wearing only hospital gowns and crying throughout the night. I wondered if she'd ever recover, ever become anything more than "Lucy in the sky with diamonds" or perhaps, in her case "without diamonds."

I found out about these patients not by talking with them but by sitting in the hallway drawing, watching and listening. Sometimes the doctor or nurses would explain things to me to encourage my participation in groups for counseling, but I never did participate. I never wanted to stand out and didn't know what to say about myself or my situation. Instead, I sat alone trying to figure out the universe and my place in it.

# Getting Ready to Leave

Time feels cold, slow and heavy when you're drugged. And I'd been drugged throughout my stay in the hospital and my time was up. I was being discharged to my mother and brother and instructed to go home to Virginia to get well. The notion was overwhelming. What on earth did it mean to be well? Had I ever been well? What would happen to me if I didn't get well? Was I well enough to know what I needed to do to get better? Like a caramel apple, now cold and turned to mush, I was trapped inside an identity disguised as someone I no longer recognized or wanted to pretend to be, an identity that may have never been anything true or real. Who I was and what I needed to do with myself in this sluggish, lifeless state was beyond comprehension.

Over that two -week period I'd watched and listened. I'd eaten well and slept. On May 31st, the date of my departure, I had come to understand the following:

1---I had to gain weight. I would be terminated from the company if I didn't, and I could possibly die.

2---I had to see a doctor regularly. This was a requirement of my employer, and without someone to guide me I was clueless as to what to do next.

3----I had to take medication the rest of my life. I was told I had a chemical condition, likely aggravated by childhood trauma, needing a chemical fix.

4---I must exercise. The rhythm of walking, the pull of the

natural environment, the stretch and contraction of muscles would have an important calming effect on my body and mind.

Along with these instructions, Dr. Wang was adamant about one more thing: I had been created in the image of God and consequently needed to live a life that reflected that. The idea was startling. I had never thought of myself in terms of God or a part of God's creation. If I thought anything, it was that I was a separate, purely physical and emotional being, a creature with no connections other than biological and cultural. The only value I had was determined by my place in society, as my mother had thought and insisted I believe. Society, not God, was the Supreme Being and I was a failed child by any criteria picked up since childhood.

My family wasn't wealthy, although we were descended from Virginia gentry. My father was an alcoholic from a family who had lost everything during the Civil War; we, as part of an unbuffered middle class, had been subject to the destabilization of the depression and the World Wars; we were not part of an established social order that offered messages of privilege and self-worth. Thus,I had come to view myself and my family as strange misfits, mostly valueless and socially unattractive. And these thoughts, because they were painful, made me angry; they needed to be disguised by social behaviors and appearances that took away the sting.

Without being able to articulate all that was rushing in and out of my altered mind, somewhere deep inside it felt as though I been drugged by destructive intoxicants; that I had been entrapped by a set of beliefs that were at war with what it meant to be whole, well and happy. I had wanted a different life from that of my parents without knowing what a different life would or could be. It wasn't about status or social standing surely. I wanted excitement, a sense of style and beauty, a life that involved flying and being free. I could imagine such a life - I had tried to live this life during my time away from home - but being a child of God hadn't crossed my mind.

Now that I was leaving the hospital, my recent mental episodes, along with the prescription, had clouded all that I had come to know about myself. I may have been shallow before my hospitalization but now I had nothing to hold on to but the words and insights of a Chinese Southern Baptist doctor.

# Going Home

**I**n retrospect: In 1964 I took off for Seattle, Washington. I had graduated from college and from stewardess school and needed a place to escape. Virginia in the 60s felt wrong for me. The ghosts my family had inherited from generation to generation combined with the not- so- subtle atmosphere of racial segregation, discrimination, and classism made me feel constrained and defenseless against a past I didn't want to be part of.

In addition, the workforce in Virginia was unaccommodating. My father who determined I not succumb to an alcoholic marriage like his own, insisted I support myself. But being a secretary, a teacher or a nurse had been the only options my mother could see and the world around me offered. And these felt too traditional to satisfy my desire for adventure and my talents for the unconventional. As an educated woman surrounded by the hopes of a new progressive era, I longed to be modern. I longed for style, possibilities and the opportunity to explore beyond the confines of a troubled past and an earlier century. Most of all, I wanted to fly.

So, in the spring of the year, I eagerly accepted a flight attendant position on the West Coast. My mother was dismayed, my father horrified, but my brother Russell, having left for the jungles of Vietnam earlier, thought it was cool. Now, ten years later, with Daddy dead from suicide, the three of us headed back home to

Virginia in a lovely modern DC-10, a super cool airplane, one I dearly loved.

I left the hospital with Momma holding tightly on to one arm and a large strong orderly holding the other. I couldn't have escaped if I'd wanted to. But my mind was on other things. Flying! I'd been told by my supervisor and the medical team that I'd be terminated unless I could prove I was fit to fly. Fit to fly? I couldn't imagine being fit for anything. But there it was, in the center of my consciousness… without flying everything would be pointless. I would be retreating to a life limited not by the sky and clouds but by attitudes of anger, frustration, illusions of success and status and the years of a large Southern family struggling with pain and abuse.

But flying was part of me, flying was hope, and during my stay at the hospital my doctor had walked me through a series of steps to get me there again: I had to go home; I had to live with my mother; I had to learn to drive so I could get to the airport where United Airlines had a base; I had to take my medicine and get healthy; and I had to see a psychiatrist on a regular basis.

Without knowing who I was, what I believed in, and how I wanted to live and why, my early adulthood had left me empty, pointless, and estranged. The things I'd been doing to get away from my past had been exciting but meaningless and destructive.

But now, even through the haze of the medication, the scattered bits and pieces of the past months were settling. My shallow, runaway thinking was being replaced with a series of steps that seemed impossible but exciting.

It was a dinner flight. After dinner the lights went out, the movie came on, and I was alone in my thoughts. The only other person whose presence I felt was the man on an aero-stretcher above me. He was hanging from the overhead bin, struggling for his life with broken bones from head to toe. There'd been a ski accident. "Get me a drink." In seconds, a gentleman in a nurse's uniform stood up with a needle in his hand. I remember thinking how lucky I was having my body intact, being able to walk off the plane on my own. As I watched the nurse give his patient a shot of sedation, it felt like I was approaching a new adventure. I fell asleep. The man above me in the aero-stretcher fell asleep. Most everyone in first class fell asleep except the flight attendants.

# My First Day Home

I was home, lying on my bed, the same bed and the same bedroom I'd slept in as a young girl. As I stared blankly at my grandmother's handmade quilt, I remember thinking how much I wanted to get up and take a walk as my doctor had told me I should. "Betsy, you have to get healthy and exercise." But nothing wanted to move. The body I'd traveled in from San Francisco wasn't mine. While the voices before the hospital stay had gone away, the drug had left me feeling heavy, numb, and separate from my desire to cooperate with my doctor.

Finally, the weight of the haze broke. It was a beautiful spring afternoon. I dressed, paused in front of the mirror to brush my dyed red hair, and slowly walked down the stairs to the familiar kitchen at the back of the house.

"I must call the doctor in Richmond," my mother said. The notion of losing my job terrified me. I'd been told I had only had three months to get well. The memories of Aunt Lena moving in and out of the State Mental Hospital; of her son going AWOL from the Korean War; of my father's suicide in the 60s; of his desperate anger and confusion throughout my childhood... at that moment all those particulars were flooded by a dark wave. The swell of panic filled my chest. I wondered if a life of broken pieces might be lost for good.

My mother lifted the phone off the wall and began dialing the number given her by Dr. Wang to Dr. Fowler who was a psychiatrist, a missionary, and a Southern Baptist like my grandmother. The conversation, just above a whisper, recounted my recent events and the need to move quickly. By the end, Dr. Fowler suggested an appointment with a doctor closer to Warrenton, Dr. Zigmund Lebensohn in D.C. She made a second call and after a short exchange looked relieved. Dr. Lebensohn could see me that week.

With the loud clacking of Dr. Scholl's sandals confirming my steps, I made my way down the asphalt driveway. After months of floating in space, it was time to take a walk. I stopped at the street and was abruptly suspended. Should I go left towards Warrenton's small shops or right towards the in-town bypass by Frost Diner? I was paralyzed even as I knew both directions and the three- mile circle they made like the back of my hand. As a girl I'd wandered these streets freely, hello-ing the people along the way, sensing them registering my family's history and mine as we casually smiled and chatted. The minutes passed. Without knowing why, I turned left and began what felt like my first deliberate walk uphill.

# Meeting Dr. Lebensohn

The day I met Dr. Lebensohn I wore a polyester blue pant suit I'd made on my Singer sewing machine in San Francisco. The pants were bell bottoms, the top was a hip length tunic, and the textured petroleum-based material was new and in vogue. I was a good seamstress as were my mother and grandmother. But on that day, as I contemplated my appearance, I was mortified. My bony physique, the brown roots of my dyed red hair, my dangling Russian earrings, my Dr. Scholls sandals, even the bright red lipstick; it all seemed wrong. I looked like a nobody left at a rural bus stop, lost and hungry.

After a breakfast of yogurt, fruit and coffee, we were off to the city in my mother's yellow AMC. The appointment was at 11:30 near Dupont Circle, an hour and a half from Warrenton. We arrived early, and for fun, happened into a magical store with the sign "Toast and Strawberrys" over the door. It turned out to be a dress and jewelry boutique specializing in locally made women's clothing, bright African dashikis, and large handmade necklaces from the other side of the globe. For fifteen or so minutes, my mind was consumed with the cheery bazaar-like atmosphere and the pleasant chatter of the African- American woman, Rosemary, who presided over her salon. Twenty years later, Rosemary and Toast and Strawberrys would remain part of my visit into the city as well as my therapy.

Nearby was Dr. Lebensohn's office, located in a lovely old building - red brick, three stories, with a small flower garden facing

R Street. We walked up two flights, passed through a large wooden door and down a short hallway. Inside his office we were greeted by an older, grey-haired woman named Mrs. Brick. She sat at a desk in front of a typewriter and as her name implied, she was rectangular and unflappable. Someone experienced with people like me, I thought. As I stood, waiting to be noticed, I pulled a flip-top case of Virginia Slims from my handbag and instantly Mrs. Brick came to life. "No smoking Miss Goin. Please go outside." I noted her dignified directness, returned the cigarette to its case and, as Mom had, took a seat on the large leather couch facing the glass top coffee table.

Within 10 minutes, Dr. Lebensohn came into the reception area. He was a small man, neatly dressed in an expensive suit and a red patterned tie. His voice was low and mellow as he greeted Mama and me. After a few words, he reached out his hand to guide me into the room on the other side of Mrs. Brick. We both sat, he behind his desk, and our conversation began.

"How are you, Miss Goin?" This first question was one he would repeat each time I saw him. How was I? I thought. And how on earth would I know. I figured he was only being polite.

"I've been better," I said.

"Tell me about that," he replied. "And why do you think you've come to see me?" The quietness of his voice and the heft of his presence softened the hard shell of my blue pantsuit. Lying, my usual strategy, wasn't an option here.

"I was told I had to see a doctor."

There was a long pause. It was hard to know what else to say.

"And why do you think you've come to see me, Miss Goin?"

Did he want to hear my recent story? Suddenly, the veneer of restraint broke loose. The words gushed out into a flood of emotion and images with no anchor in sight. Who was speaking? I wondered. But I didn't care or interrupt as I hovered over myself, watching the two of us: the curious red headed woman telling tales of spaceships, planes and jumping off bridges and Dr. Lebensohn, taking notes and patiently observing.

Our time together was almost up. And then he dropped the bomb.

"Miss Goin, what do YOU want to do?"

The question was implausible. I? Me? What did I want to do?" I'd never been asked such a question or even contemplated options. Flying had been the only possibility, flying as a career choice. But Dr. Lebensohn was asking about me, the inner me, the person not the worker, not the woman who had to support herself so she wouldn't have to be unhappily married. There was no relevancy or capacity to respond, only numbness. And Dr. Lebensohn must have sensed this. So, he continued.

"Yes, Miss Goin, what do YOU want to do?"

# A Stake in the Ground

As Dr. Lebensohn's words crossed over the desk, my fingers pressed into cool brown leather. My cheeks grew warmer. I wasn't accustomed to telling the truth. Truth wasn't in my repertoire. And yet now my livelihood and independence depended on it. On one hand I wanted to cooperate. After all he was trying to help me and might soon get tired of listening if I lied. On the other, his question made me angry. I was used to reacting spontaneously and not having to think. But now I was forced to look inward to see what I could find. Red tie, leather chair, blue pant suit, Toast and Strawberries. The facts were inaccessible, and I felt stupid. There was little I could say so I avoided the question. And yet Dr. Lebensohn continued to look at me with a patience I'd never known before.

"What do you want to do, Miss Goin?"

It took months before I could offer a sincere answer.

Once a week, I would enter his office and be confronted by his persistence, "How are you, Miss Goin?" Week after week, I hoped something meaningful would emerge as I jabbered on about books, painting, music, dance, activities and details that had busied my life. Sometimes he would mention his family. I never mentioned mine. And as the weeks progressed, I continued to worry he would send me off to someone else; that I wasn't a good enough patient for him and wasting his time.

But during this first visit, our conversation had resulted in something that seemed like progress. After 45 minutes, somehow an official diagnosis of my scary behavior of the past months, even years, had emerged and was now in print. The courier type on the bill said it all, "Acute Schizophrenic Episode, Paranoid Variety in Remission." Unlike those frantic sensations that had pulled me deep into my illness, I now had a determination on paper that felt tangible and calm. The paper confirmed that I was no longer hearing voices and yet I was acutely mentally ill. Together, Dr. Lebensohn and I had plunged a stake in the ground. And as I walked down the stairs to the garden below, I wondered what was next.

# The Church of Granny Russell

During the week after my appointment, I slept, ate and went for daily walks. I was still taking a large dose of medication and it was the medication that had become my sense of self. I had little inside to anchor me naturally or to coax me into normal adult activities. And because of the medication or because there was no real me inside, I didn't talk. I had nothing to say and so chose to keep to myself.

Only when my mother asked specific questions did I converse. Over the phone I'd talk to my cousin. We'd talk about the upscale bargains from D.C. department stores she wore to her job as a secretary at an international organization. As I listened, it felt good to feel less of a misfit. To her I wasn't lost, merely an offbeat who had taken a different path from more conservative, less adventurous types. I enjoyed imagining her bright blue eyes caked in eyeshadow lighting up as I'd tell her my stories of life between San Francisco and Hawaii. The satisfaction of her viewing my life as cool and exciting relieved my sense of medicated dullness. Our experiences of life created a bond.

And then there was my grandmother, Granny Russell. Immediately after I returned to Virginia, she began to spend purposeful time with me, picking me up in Warrenton and taking me to her house 35 miles away in Falls Church, where she lived alone with a roomer who came and went as he pleased. Granny Russell, my mother's mother, was an accomplished homemaker, seamstress and widow. She was also a committed Southern Baptist. It was during my stays with Granny that I became aware of why she'd reached out to me. She imagined her non-speaking and non-believing granddaughter deserved far better and she needed to help. And she did help. She picked up where Dr. Wang left off, encouraging me to think about my life and my body in positive ways, encouraging me to consider that there was something special about me, something put there by her Baptist-loving God that she wanted me to find.

Most importantly to my sensibilities, Granny was a devoted shopper and TV watcher. With the enthusiasm of an evangelist, she'd drive me to Tyson's Corner, the biggest mall in the area, to browse dresses at Woodies and then lunch at the new French crepe shop, The Magic Pan. At 3 p.m. each afternoon, she'd hand me a cold glass of sweetened tea and together, from her living room coach, we'd watch her favorite soap opera, "General Hospital", differentiating characters and life styles - good from bad, troubled from innocent - as she whispered out the nuances gathered from her time as a fan.

It was during this time with Granny that I began to speak openly again. My days gardening with her in her back yard, taking walks around the flower-filled neighborhood, preparing simple dinners together, chatting over our shared readings from the Bible, helping her imagine patterns from the silky, tight-fitting fashions we watched on afternoon TV; all these things began to divert my attention from the emptiness and confusion I felt. Granny Russell's "Church of the General Hospital" provided friendship, compassion, and a real and fictionalized morality play I could watch and internalize. It connected me to people and personalities, intentions and hopes, values and traits, truths and consequences. Rather than diverting me from life, its interwoven stories and characters allowed me to pull from the matrix a small but intact personhood, a sense of heft inside I'd never felt before. Despite the confusion, the doubt, and the fog of heavy medication, Granny Russell's love and wisdom created a space for me to discover something new.

# Taffy and the Lava Lamp

During the months of June and July, I was busy.

One day a week, I'd make an all- day trip to see Dr. Lebensohn. I'd begin the day around 6 a.m. walking to the Grey Hound Station not far from the Warrenton Horse Show grounds and about a mile and a half from my mother's house. The bus was mostly filled with domestic help making their way from rural Virginia to the mansions in Georgetown and the northwest corridors of D.C. I was one of the few white people and one of the many women. As we rode along, I'd watch the countryside turn from pastures to suburbia to white monuments along the Potomac and anger would well up in me. I was no longer in San Francisco; the city on the Bay that offered independence, beauty and a dream of becoming someone else.

But on the bus, while alternating napping and listening, I was able to relax into the rhythm of the female ridership - their stories of misbehaving children, haughty employers, broken-down cars and relationships, all fodder for belly-aching jokes and free flowing comradery. I felt in their simple kindness towards me a welcome warmth. The long, slow trip lifted me into an unfamiliar experience of acceptance, and I'd fall back asleep.

By early morning, we'd arrive downtown. The walk to Dupont Circle would take almost two hours as I stopped along the way, first at the Mayflower Hotel for a cup of coffee and fruit and then by Kramer Books for browsing among the mystery, sci-fi and humor selections. If there was time, I'd visit Rosemary, owner of Toast and

Strawberries, wander among her clothes and jewelry, hear about her important community work, and often get introduced to local designers and craft people - all artsy, confident, and full of urban attitude. I remember chatting happily with them, enjoying the distance away from hard and troubled thinking.

At a little before 11:30 a.m., I'd purchase a second cup of coffee on Connecticut Avenue and begin the final path to my appointment with a pleasant lilt to my steps. Then, after 45 minutes, my time with Dr. Lebensohn was up and, in his fatherly manner, he'd escort me out, and I'd window shop back to the bus station by way of the art galleries on the Mall. Like my days as a stewardess, I'd walk alone among art galleries and gardens, enjoy an early and simple dinner and then join my companions for a quiet ride home. The satisfaction of being alone and free, of being a quiet but watchful presence among paintings, sculpture, and sober spaces had prepared me for the week's work ahead.

The days I traveled to D.C. were always an adventure. The rest of the week I was faced with the reality of living with an incurable disease called mental illness.

My disease, I'd learned from Dr. Lebensohn, was just that, not a death sentence, not a social disgrace, not something to reduce my feeling of self-worth. It was very similar, he said, to his own heart condition, a chronic obstruction to his tennis game that required medication and special attention but not a serious one. That's what he'd told me.

The truth was my episode and need for psychiatric help made me feel inferior, hollow and deeply sad. Of course, I'd always felt inferior: being short, not prone to a thin, model-like figure, having bad hair, being from a questionable family, not fitting in with the Warrenton Jones'. Now I had a new reason to feel bad about myself and so I did. I couldn't stretch myself taller as I'd attempted in my teens, attaching feet and hands to my four -poster bed. As someone with mental illness, what could I possibly do to become 'normal?' And what was 'normal?' It was up to me to figure this out.

As for the hollowness, that wasn't a new sensation either. I just hadn't paid much attention to it, and thought it was how most people felt. When I considered my identity, I conceived of myself as skin surrounding hot air; no bones, organs or muscles, just a vague, dark, substance-less space. Rather than that being troubling, it had made me feel lighter, less restricted, separate from the confined physical dimension and separate from others.

And the sadness, that had been a part of me since childhood as well. Experiences of watching my father drink himself into a stranger colored my home life dark and lonely. One moment he'd talk to me about my education, my future, my interests in art and reading. He'd encourage me to take part in school activities and spoke about the importance of being self-reliant. "Betsy, I want you to go to college so you won't have to rely on someone to take care of you." Hours later after bourbon and beers, he'd become unrecognizable.

As a teenager, I reacted to my home relationships and immediate surroundings with deep sadness and confusion Something was not right with me, I thought. Whoever I was deep inside didn't live there. The person who might have lived down there was neither home nor happy. Home, after all, where a child should feel comfortable and secure, had abandoned me. Instead of wanting to be at home in myself, I busied myself with activities, pursued almost anything that might let me feel free and independent from the nagging sensation inside, and wore a mask to ensure the world and myself that I was worthy even as a sense of homelessness resided below my heart. The sense of self into which I had retreated had claimed my ability to focus, to plow a pathway for escaping the homelessness inside.

When I started therapy, something told me to dump everything I knew about how I should live, that all the cues I'd picked up from school, family, work, church were suspect and no longer valid or relevant. And of course, many of them weren't: the racism, the inequality between the sexes, my parents' tumultuous marriage and parenting, our government's involvement in Vietnam. The norms and institutions of my past and present had all failed me. Yet I had to find a new source for creating myself, for balancing the hot air, that deep ache inside, with external substance and a persona.

So, I became a people watcher. I began looking for clues as to what I should be looking and acting like. I watched television: General Hospital, Star Trek, Columbo, special programs with Billy Graham; and I watched people along the street.

When I went to the store, I observed how people shopped, how they talked to their children, their spouses and the clerks. When I went to the bank, I noticed how long people took making deposits, chatting with tellers about their busy day and their need to get back to work. On the weekends, my mother took me to farm fairs, art shows and local social outings. Her commitment to keeping me socialized and active, as Dr. Lebensohn had encouraged, gave me content for imagining a life.

After weeks of observations, something became clear to me: most people are busy; most people are moving from one activity to the next; most people are tied to a way of life that doesn't allow them to focus on the purpose of their life; and most people, unlike me I thought, could easily move forward with the life they'd been given. And that was the difference: I no longer had a life to live that was in any way easy or acceptable; that gave me a foundation and connection with others that, if not totally positive, was at least not doomed for a speedy and frightening demise. My life in San Francisco prior to my break down was an indication I no longer had a past that could lead me forward and keep me alive. My unacceptability had not only been fully demonstrated but officially spotted and labeled. According to the authorities at United and confirmed by my San Francisco doctors, it was impossible for me to work and be independent again until my life, its values, assumptions and behaviors, had been influenced by a degree of sanity I might have never had.

Now that I was unemployed, free from imposed schedules, free from my questionable friends in San Francisco and not restricted during the week by my mother's "get Betsy out of the house and socialized" push, I had the time and strong inclination to try to figure things out; things like: what characteristics did I need to pursue to get away from the destructive life style I had fled to in my dissolute 20s?

The responsibility of a transformation when there was nothing to start with overwhelmed me, weighed me down, and immobilized me with feelings of anxiety. For hours, I'd be stuck staring at a blank TV screen, staring at the striped red and beige wallpaper in my mother's living room, feeling the effects of my mind slowly churning the state of my unacceptability, replaying the numbing inconclusiveness over and over inside my head. Who did I need to become? What was real? The boredom of not knowing became palpable. Like the summer heat, it settled into my warm clammy skin, softening me, like overripe camembert, into a place where thoughts merge into wordlessness, flowing like the shapes and colors of an amorphous Lava Lamp, replacing the mantra of doubt and doom with mindlessness. And then the body of a white Cocker Spaniel named Taffy would spread across my lap. I'd feel his nose nudging into my side. I'd sense his spirit, hear his kindness and hold his devotion to human exchange against my heart. This was real, I thought. Slowly I began to kick-start a life by opening myself to the universe.

# From the Debris

When you've hit rock bottom how do you start anew? My rock bottom had brought everything into question and had caused me to throw out every assumption that had governed my life. The person that had allowed me to attend school, to barely graduate from college, to become a flight attendant, to move to San Francisco had been grounded in a theory of being that I could no longer trust. My theory of being had been derived from a small life with little instruction other than "look and act like you are somebody, do what you can to enjoy yourself." So I did, living my part with no concept as to why it all mattered.

At the big level, I was struck by the dynamics playing out in society during the 60s to the point of being more than just concerned and angry. The news of the day called upon me to emotionally identify with the underclass, those living unprotected lives, with few rights or resources to help them maneuver the challenges of getting an education, finding a job, keeping their health, raising whole families. I'd think about the young men drafted into a war for reasons most of us didn't understand, with those suffering from the racism and violence that plagued the inner cities and southern towns, and with the voices of women raising issues about sexual inequality and lack of political, financial and social respect.

At the personal level, I was unable to connect to the people I worked and lived with every day. Much of this was aggravated by alcohol. Alcohol was available to my teenage friends easily back then and many of their parents were alcoholic, depressed and stressed. Back then, there was no public awareness of the connection of alcohol to car accidents or mental health. Alcohol, not drugs, was the seductive mask of choice. My relationships, established through local social gatherings, helped to strengthen the barrier I felt with others, a barrier disguised with attitudes of a happy coolness that identified me and my friends as members of an imaginary "In" crowd. And being in this "In" crowd meant I had to look better, act better, and successfully compete with others so the shallowness I felt would stay appropriately anesthetized. Threats from my father kept me from drinking, but the pickled persona of others limited my friendships to the superficial and removed and modeled for me a set of behaviors and attitudes I assumed was normal.

Even without alcohol, my brain was strained and awkward. Its response to life was primarily visual and intellectual, taking information in, analyzing it, judging it, absorbing what seemed good, rejecting what seemed bad and orchestrating a young life from the debris around me. As part of the debris, I felt like isolated riffraff yet talked through an impersonation of someone who could fake themselves into happiness. Instead of being able to think and act from a place inside that I identified as "I" or "Me," I thought and acted on behalf of "She," "Her" or "It." These pronouns likely came about from my early schizophrenic tendencies, perhaps a chemical imbalance that encouraged my brain to divorce my physical self from my body and inner spiritual life, from my sensing and thinking self. Out of unconscious desperation, I had created a woman who chose to be cool, competent, and oblivious of the consequences of an imitated, isolated, abstract, and ungrounded life. And when the disguise was lost, she was lost.

There were two points that marked my early journey through mental illness: the point at which I realized I was lost, and the point at which I realized I was a fake.

The first one came about during my hospital stay in San Francisco. I not only came to see that I had no bearings or pathway forward. I started to question my preference for solitude and fantasy. I began to understand that living in a world of my own making with science fiction as the core reality was scary and destructive. In addition, I was anorexic, suffering from the pain and confusion of a broken heart, overcome by a run of the mill nervous breakdown, and under the constant stress of holding onto a challenging job and a deadly relationship while moving deeper into psychoses. Call it what you want to, I was in trouble and lost.

The second point came about while in my first several months of psychotherapy with Dr. Lebensohn. Although I'd not developed the insight to know this, my deeper "real" self had been taught to retreat in order to protect itself from criticism and harm, both physical and psychological. As a result, I'd grown another self, one that could face up to what my family and the perceived social order around me could accept, maybe even admire and recognize as different and special. You might say that the second self was put together with baling wire and papier mache: a set of values made from the need to be attractive, a set of relationships with men and women who were interesting and good-looking, a job that was responsible so others could think of me as a grown up and not the injured and homeless child inside.

Somewhere inside I was compassionate. It expressed itself when the news media focused my attention on those mistreated and misunderstood. But my created self had no room for compassion. Worrying about how others felt and feeling empathy for them as friends or love interests was outside of the realm of my fake persona. The energy I might have used to really care about someone needed to be spent holding myself together. It was Dr. Lebensohn's question, "Miss Goin what do you want to do" combined with the realization of how lost I had become that helped me realize that there might be an "I" buried beneath the mess of my unhappy world.

# Starship Gremlin

So how do you find a sense of purpose and self-worth when you are fake? I bought a car. The saved money was set aside from my earlier paychecks as a flight attendant. As mentally challenged as I was at the time, I knew how to hold onto a dollar. My only real expenses in San Francisco were the rent for a small apartment with rent control, a few nice clothes to supplement my uniforms, and books. I had a library of books from Russian novels, authors from the American South to science fiction. Because my work involved traveling and exploring new cities, there was no need to spend on outside entertainment. Painting and reading books and an occasional purchase let me live cheaply. In addition to having the entire price of a new car in the bank, I was able to help my mother pay the bills of living in her own house on a main street in Warrenton.

After returning to Warrenton, one of my first acts of whosesomeness was to get my driver's license. Soon after, my mother and I hopped into her car and drove the 25 miles to the AMC dealership in Manassas. Proudly, I returned home with a shiny Purple Gremlin resembling a spaceship, identifying me as modern and adventurous. On the rear bumper, I attached a "Beam Me Up Scotty" sticker. The excitement of having my own transportation was only outweighed by my fear of driving on the road. I had passed the test to drive with my mother's help, but my lack of experience combined with my medication and a heavy foot ensured a feeling of wild instability. I was a she-devil on wheels. Panicked but persistent, with a slightly plumper and less anorexic profile, my first adventure was into the deep suburbs. Over the several months of being at home, I had gained weight. My blue jeans and shirts were too snug to be attractive, so I needed new ones. By myself and in my new Gremlin, I found my way down 66, merged onto the inner beltway of 495 around D.C., navigated the huge Tysons Corner Mall, and returned to Warrenton safely before dark. The accomplishment was worthy of the crew of Star Trek. With my new clothes and my small purple car inspiring me, I felt ready to "go where no one had gone before."

# The Four Doctors

Soon after I'd bought my new car, two things happened. Dr. Lebensohn lowered my medication to as low a dosage as possible, and my three- month medical leave of absence was up.

The low dosage was to prevent severe side effects such as tardive dyskinesias, which causes involuntary movements of the mouth and face; excessive and unhealthy weight gain; and dry mouth which makes sound sleep difficult and causes dental problems. Fortunately, only the dry month problem persisted under the lower dosage and even today I struggle with waking up unable to swallow.

The three- month leave was the time I'd been given by United to restore my sanity. My agreement required passing interviews with four doctors before I could start work again. During one week in mid-August, I drove in to D.C. for my first evaluation with Dr. Lebensohn, my personal psychiatrist, and then flew to San Francisco for an interview with both Dr. Wang, the psychiatrist who had treated me when I was in the hospital, and Dr. Schwartz, a medical director with United. When I came back from San Francisco, I met with Dr. Finelle, another United medical director in Washington D.C.

I remember walking in to meet with each of these gentlemen feeling like a quiet and polite zombie. I was looking much better, having gained a few pounds, with my hair one color, and wearing a summer weight linen suit with two -inch heels. In addition to the Revlon China-glaze Red lipstick and discrete eye makeup, my face had now cleared up. No more adult acne as I'd been fighting since my early twenties. I was pleased I didn't look like a beatnik, as I had at one time, but I felt artificial and frozen as I took my seat on their judgement stands. Once settled, however, my gift of gab kicked in, and with one or two questions from the doctors I was off, carrying on a conversation that any first -class passenger and my mother would have been pleased with.

Each doctor seemed remarkably kind to me. I was likely the first United employee with schizophrenia that any of these men had ever had to interview who wanted to return to work.

Without much discussion, the youngest doctor of the four focused on marriage and wondered why I would want to go back to work. "If it's marriage you're looking for, you're good looking enough to be able to find a man on your own Miss Goin." He seemed puzzled that a thirty-two- year old "older woman" would want to start back to work after three months off. I was too focused on trying to get my job back to be upset by his view of women.

The other United doctor could only imagine I'd been on drugs. He was from San Francisco of course. Fortunately,my appearance seemed contrary to a typical 60s' West Coast drug user and my demeanor was more polished and focused than the sedated women from the Valley of the Dolls. Despite the discomfort of trying to answer his probing questions while fighting the faint but annoying fog of medication, by the end of the interview he, along with the others, told me he'd be recommending reinstatement. The mask of a stewardess, always smiling, nodding, and acting polite and non-threatening, served me well.

By the first of September my life had turned a corner again. I received a letter from the Personnel Office letting me know I would remain on probation and be stationed in D.C. for six months and would soon be scheduled for my first flight. Unbelievable! While still feeling sick with no place to go, I could now return to my love of flying and my skill at living and working behind my mask.

# Back to Work

I remember a few things about my first day returning to work. It was September 11th,1974 and a gorgeous day. I was dressed in one of my old uniforms, a mid-night blue jumper with a polka dot shirt. And it occurred to me on the way to the airport that driving my car into the local gravel quarry off Rt. 29 would be easier than facing the first day of my new life, the day I was to meet my new flight crew, my new supervisor, and then fly off to San Francisco. For moments, suicide seemed easier. I would be free of the responsibility of getting back on my feet, free of all the colleagues and supervisors talking behind my back, free of being the red- headed woman who required a three- month mental health break and probably shouldn't be trusted. I was clearly unsure of myself and after I parked my Gremlin and walked across the Dulles tarmac, I entered the United Airlines office scared to death.

Strangely, I thought, my supervisor's first words to me were "How are you feeling?" I don't remember replying. He then added, "You know you're on probation."

Fortunately, many of the crew members were old acquaintances from the mid-60s when I was based in Washington. I immediately felt comfortable with them as we exchanged hellos and a few introductions. But soon we were off on my first flight after being in the hospital and I was terrified again. I was sure I might do something wrong. My personality was still traumatized from all I'd been through. Perhaps my dark voices would come back, perhaps they would tell me to upset the passengers, pour coffee on their heads, open an emergency door and leap into thin air. The possibilities seemed endless as I carefully tried to follow the steps and procedures highlighted during our crew's briefing.

I tried to imagine myself as a normal and responsible person. The message of Peale's "The Power of Positive Thinking" buttressed my thoughts. I looked around the cabin for clues from the other stewardesses and worked hard at following them. Time passed. The food and drinks were dispersed without incident, and the movie – thankfully uninterrupted by flying space aliens - softened the long trip.

Once we landed, I hopped into a van and in fifteen minutes arrived at the Benjamin Franklin Hotel in San Mateo. The flight had been stressful, and when stressed I take a long walk or go shopping. Immediately after carrying my one small suitcase and tote bag to my room, I headed back down the elevator to walk along El Camino Real, a large heavily trafficked avenue I'd visited many times before. For miles I walked, my mind absorbed by the blue California sky, the cream- colored buildings, the concrete sidewalks, and the drone of shiny cars zipping along side me. And then, after 2½ miles, I arrived: an expansive shopping mall with a Nordstrom's and a food court, my reward for an eventful day. Finally, I could be at peace with myself: the colorful clothes, the modern shoes, the bustling people with interesting faces. The arcs and flows of outside stimulation mellowed my war- torn brain.

# *Advice for Good Living*

Just as my first outward bound flight was uneventful, so was my flight back home. No voices demanding that I cause a commotion, no inclination to shift a sleeping man's toupees or dribble red wine on a haughty woman's bosom. My medication must have been doing its job. Or perhaps my schizophrenic episode was just that: a single episode.

But regardless of any permanent chemical imbalance, I'd been so frightened by my loss of control and frequent states of paranoia that now, back on the job, it felt comforting to know I was seeing a doctor who I trusted like no one else. I had a father figure. And I had a relationship with a kind and brilliant man who made me feel I was doing something important for myself by following his advice, who offered me the chance of becoming someone who might be perceived as normal.

When I met with Dr. Lebensohn, he never spent time delving into my past. He was most concerned on the here and now; helping me know how to get through one day at a time and how to interact with people.

Back then, I was most comfortable being alone, separate from everything other than my own thoughts and imagination. I wallowed in them. Dr. Lebensohn, realizing this, insisted I pull away from activities that would submerge me into my trance like state of fantasy and isolation. He wanted to instill in me an approach to life that would lift me out of my seclusion, physically and mentally. He gave me specific directions and his character and intellect inspired me to follow his lead. Here's a partial list of his instructions including his very words burned into my mind by his powerful and hypnotic voice.

"Don't read or watch science fiction." Science fiction can pull those overly attracted to fantasy away from our current surroundings and opportunities. It can elevate us into a sense of wonder with things unknown and diminishes the importance of our daily lives. Watching Star Trek is ok because the plots are about basic human hopes and values. Star Trek can inspire us and enable us to distinguish good choices from bad.

"Find an opportunity to be around people every day." Getting to know people, sharing thoughts and ideas with them helps to build compassion and a feeling of being part of a community, even if a small one.

"Learn more about and seek out your religious heritage." People with mental illness do better if they root themselves in their faith tradition, giving them a greater feeling of self-worth and meaning.

"Pursue creative interests." Doing art, music, writing, woodworking, a range of things helps to channel hidden thoughts and ideas that are not easily expressed through other means. It helps us feel pride and greater positive self-awareness.

"Find an interest and learn more about it." In doing so, attend classes where you can learn with others and discover how interests can be shared and further developed.

"Exercise often." Physical activity makes you feel better in all ways while it also alleviates pain and weight issues.

"Engage in yoga and meditation." Focusing and quieting the mind helps provide a space for healing and centeredness. The disquieted mind can cause unnecessary stress and disillusionment.

"Let yourself be sad and lonely if that's how you're feeling." Indulge in this sadness for a set amount of time - no more than a half an hour. When you become bored with that, move on. Read a good book, watch a good TV program, attend an interesting movie or play to help you get out of your sadness and get on with your life.

"Learn how to present yourself in a positive way." Feel pride in how you look and realize that how you take care of yourself can make a positive impression on others as well as help you connect with them. (This is an old tradition that dates to cave men and women.)

"Don't eat too much and eat healthily with lots of vegetables and good fats." Sugary soft drinks, packaged snack foods, and empty carbohydrates make you sick.

"Consume little liquor and no illegal drugs." Don't risk the consequences of too much alcohol to your physical and mental health.

These instructions were shared with me over many months. Further elaborating and assisting with how to use them took many years. But as of September 1974, the initial outline was my bridge and passage- way. It provided a means for learning how to become a member of society again, of how to return to my position with United and an independent life. I held onto them as pilings in a swamp filled with alligators.

# Starting on the Path

D r. Lebensohn told me repeatedly that having a serious illness can be a blessing in disguise; it can help you realize how essential it is to take care of your basic needs and requirements. So with my first flight as "Betsy who has schizophrenia" out of my way and a growing sense of confidence, I began to focus my attention on Dr. Lebensohn's "prescriptions."

I started with acquainting myself with religion. It happened by accident when my grandmother, an ardent Southern Baptist whose genetic mean streak had been nicely modified by her church-biding willingness to help people, invited me once again to go to church with her. I was hesitant. Church going would require I be around lots of people. Lots of people would then get to know my business. It also would require that I set aside time each week to attend. I didn't have lots of time. My medication was still causing me to take multiple naps during the day and I needed my walks and occasional shopping sprees to keep my stress level under control. It all seemed like an inconvenience and an annoyance, but I had to give it a try.

Both Dr. Wang and Grannie Green had instilled in me that I needed to consider myself as a child of God with inherent worth. The point of view, although force-fed, seemed refreshing. I was tired of being a frightened valueless nobody, turning exclusively to external sources to secure an identity and gain validation. Things like trendy clothes, parties, movies, all sort of life- style activities without any perspective to provide a foundation or grounding had left me feeling hollow and bored. Pointless. And this pointlessness was oppressive. Having inherent worth was a curiosity, something new to think about and possibly a way to feel better about myself. But following my devoted Grandmother's lead to the Southern Baptists was not an option. As someone inclined to privacy and introversion, I needed a church and congregation to be quiet and reflective. After all, I was on medication to ensure my emotions were under control. The Baptists, on the other hand, were into emotion, more than I could possibly stand. And, more importantly, many Baptists, like Grannie, didn't believe in predestination. I did. Deep inside, starting as a child, I knew my path had been established. Without any outside direction, I was convinced a divine force had something in store for me. That memorable day in San Francisco, trying to burn my Bible in the kitchen in order to incite God's wrath and my execution, was proof. I should have died, and I didn't. Someone intervened. Instead of receiving a fatal punishment, I was faced with cleaning up a mess of ashes and charred wallpaper and the possibility I needed help.

So Granny, Mom and I drove off to service with the Presbyterians, a compromise with no prospect of turning into a commitment. I was sure of it. I would attend church, try out religion and report back to Dr. Lebensohn that I was being a cooperative patient. By attending the coffee and cookie "Refreshment" part of the service, I would get credit for another item on his prescribed list: being around people and talking with them. Grannie would step into a house of heathens in order to support me and my mother would go along for the ride, eager to meet and greet whoever she could.

The old brick church was filled. We found a seat in the back, close to the exit and next to no one I knew and soon one thing followed another: several prayers, a reading from the Bible, hymns, a sermon I don't remember, and a feeling of impatience and restlessness. As we came into the home stretch, Mrs. Jones, the organist, began her final piece. She pressed on the pedals, pulled out the stops and, with magic in her fingertips, filled the room with Christian revelation. The hymn "Great Is Thy Faithfulness," was nothing I had ever heard before. But, within seconds, its early last century earnestness hit me like a ton of bricks. The congregation sang full throttle and I, without hesitation, did as well, leaving all self-consciousness behind, losing myself in the moment, and letting the emotion of being loved and cared for penetrate my bones. Perhaps this was what Dr. Lebensohn was talking about.

# *Feeling Happy*

The church experience made me feel happy. And happiness had never been part of any outcome I'd hoped for. Instead, my twenties had been spent doing things that were darkly interesting: watching Ingmar Bergman movies, reading Ibsen, Dostoyevsky, and Faulkner; and talking fashionable philosophy, like existentialism and relativism, with semi-intellectual kids and young adults high on alcohol and the desire to be perceived as cool.

The times were dark too. World War II had only recently passed, the assassinations of the two Kennedy's, Martin Luther King, and Malcolm X had happened in a span of five years, the Vietnam War was in full force and the overshadowing effects of Camelot were long gone. With the dull and constant changes caused by integration, the sexual revolution, and the God is Dead movement, and with the rising numbers of those in poverty in America and those dead on the battlefield and from heroin in the back streets, Life Magazine, the premier journal of the times, portrayed the world as being heavy, hard and darkly beautiful.

Happiness seemed to me and many others my age to be both silly and old-fashioned. More appreciated, trendy emotions - lacking any sweetness or innocence - were the newly minted and marketed sentiments of cool and funky. The moments approaching happiness that I remember were those looking through edgy fashion magazines with bold colored photos of big- eyed Twiggy - the supermodel of the 60s - wearing magical outfits with white plastic go-go boots, finding a doctor to prescribe birth control pills, piercing one's ears to wear hoops, attending large concerts to dance in the aisles. It was as if a new order had taken over the hearts and minds of a generation. And the order was aligned with a cold and angular aesthetic that hummed to the sound of electric guitars and the clean perfection of science and science fiction. Traditional happiness seemed too much rooted in the past and the long skirts, the modest hats and suede cotton gloves my mother wore to show off that she was somebody, refined and rightly born. Traditional happiness, from the viewpoint of my generation, was something that belonged in parish halls, social teas, debutante parties, cocktail hours and other places that beckoned back to the norms of a white society based on class, status and reflected in the movies.

But on that Sunday morning I left the church feeling that the dark universe had lost its hold. And as I walked down the sidewalk with my mother and Granny, something that felt like the love and forgiveness of a God I'd never known or acknowledged before seemed to walk alongside me.

Religion touched a nerve that day and I began going to church on a regular basis, enjoying the music, contemplating the sermons, participating in Bible studies, and attempting to sing in the choir with a voice that didn't belong there.

But church was only one item on Dr. Lebensohn's list. The requirement to involve myself in art and creativity was another. So soon after my church experience, I began taking art lessons at the local community college with a teacher named Randy. And I loved it. The building was brand new and beautiful. The teacher was a gifted instructor who had a knack for finding out people's unique style and encouraging it with enthusiasm. Going to class with Randy at the helm provided stimulation, emotional support, and a community of artsy people, old and young, who I enjoyed watching, learning from, and getting to know.

As an Arts major in college, I'd been surrounded by suburban white kids with a similar but limited point of view. At the community college, people from all walks of life were represented. Their unfamiliar and unpredictable attitudes and approaches to art and life fascinated me. For the first time, I had friends who were black, Asian, Muslim, retired, pretending to be hippies, former convicts, the whole gamut. And most everyone wore the same blue jeans as I did.

While work with my fellow flight attendants reminded me I could once again hold a job and support myself, my time in art class became another church experience, helping me feel I was more than just an employee on probation trying to get back on her feet.

Art classes and working on my paintings helped me understand how I saw the world. When painting, I learned that I preferred two dimensions. Rather than attempting to imitate a traditional view of the world or to copy the world I saw with my eyes, I enjoyed creating my own space with shapes, colors, edges and lines, and bringing into existence things I controlled through brushwork and colors.

Creating flatness on canvas felt more interesting and more authentic. By doing so, my pictures became inventions from somewhere inside me, not reproductions of things others saw or experienced. By letting my meditative mind - and I seemed to paint best in a trance-like state - put one stroke and one color next to another, I made paintings that manifested things I could not say or explain.

Unfortunately, these exhibitions of my inner world could only be loved my mother, brother or teacher that wished to see the best in me. Others, more removed and critical, and those who might have been looking for beauty or a compliment to their interior decor, were disappointed if not horrified. Consequently, my paintings rarely sold. My art was not commercial. Instead, it was as much about creating magic as it was therapy. And my magic was only for me. In the Warrenton area, if I had focused on perfecting the head and body of a fox or a thoroughbred, I would have been successful. Instead, my cats, people, houses, flowers and vases collected themselves onto canvases that lined the walls of my mother's garage, my studio.

# Brush Strokes

During the first year of painting with Randy, my brush strokes and colors evolved. I would move from periods of trance-like painting in my mother's poorly lit garage to being a focused student in the sunlit classroom and wonder how on earth I saw things the way I did. When I produced one three- armed rendering of a fellow flight attendant and used thick cadmium orange to represent the black hair of another, I felt liberated and pleased with the effects. While I was no Matisse, I was unconsciously following in the steps of a painter who might have understood my need to move through the literal world into a realm of mad but calculated visualization. I was spitting things onto my canvases, transferring confusing sensations into expressions that met my own criteria for harmony and proportion. I used the flat surfaces to anchor my wild, uncontrollable spinnings to a more manageable realm where they settled amidst colors and textures not normally associated with tasteful art. If people enjoyed my work, I was thrilled but that only occurred by accident.

It was only much later that I became interested in subjects outside myself; things like flowers, vases and even horses; interesting shapes that I used to create movement on canvas through contrasting colors, lines and brush strokes. And as Randy encouraged me to explore a range of tones and hues, my flatness became tinged with space and depth.

It was during my early flat period that I met Robyn. I had

been encouraged by Dr. Lebensohn to find outlets for a spiritual life and my creativity. Now he insisted I address my preference for my own company and long bouts contemplating Star Trek jigsaw puzzles. These were triggers for isolation, loneliness and more mental health problems he believed. So, after starting church and attending art classes, I responded to the velvet-voiced requirement of Dr. Lebensohn and forced myself to look for people with whom I could have a conversation. The odds were against me I thought. Finding anyone interesting and relatable in the small town of Warrenton seemed unlikely. My life before and during my hospitalization had set me apart, made me someone estranged from more normal people, more normal small -town people I was someone who had been directed by inner voices, wired to flying saucers, assured that the stars had been rearranged by space aliens. I also was an active and inquiring reader, someone with an intellect and an education, someone who had studied and admired great thinkers and artists. I had both an active inner life that was other worldly and seriously flawed and one rooted in the best our planet had to offer. It was while drawing people on the streets of Warrenton that I was introduced to the idea of meeting the new owner of the Town Duck.

# Meeting at the Town Duck

The main street of Warrenton in the 70s was patronized by the same kind of customers that had shopped there as far back as the 40s. There was Carter's, a dimly lit clothing store with tables of folded pants and shirts specializing in a brand of blue jeans that most local farmers and the hardworking horsey set had to have; two hardware stores that had expanded into kitchen wares and overstuffed sofas for the owners of new ramblers built around town during the 50s, Sweeney's, a well-stocked shoe store that included Bass Weejuns, PF Flyers and expensive shoes for Warrenton's better dressed; and two drug stores including Rhode's with a lunch counter offering sundaes, grilled cheese sandwiches, and a comfortable meeting place for all. The only fancy store in town was Hurst Jewelers where well-heeled locals purchased their engagement rings, formal dinner china and sterling flatware.

The new Town Duck was different. The offerings included unique food items such as specialty cheeses and crackers and wines, funky tchotchkes and humorous art pieces, colorful tea towels and aprons, and expensive French cookware. As Warrenton had grown and changed, the Town Duck in the 70s was becoming a refuge for those imagining a life beyond their tractors and horse trailers. I was fascinated.

From my walks back and forth into Warrenton on drawing expeditions, I'd grown to admire what looked like exotic still-lives in the store's two display windows. One day I noticed a white and blue vase there, modern and elegant... I ventured inside. To my surprise, the young owner greeted me politely and we began to talk. Robyn was in her early twenties then, small with a beautiful long braid down her back and an open and lively way of presenting herself; a flower child in sweatpants I could relate to. And I wanted her to relate to me, an artist, I told her, trying to get back on my feet, a modern painter with an eye for detail who had recently escaped from a schizophrenic episode in San Francisco and now was earning a living serving coffee and cocktails across the friendly skies.

As I shared all this mindlessly, Robyn looked at me as if I was a normal and interesting person. For the first time in a long time, that's almost how I felt: normal in an artsy kind of way. As I gathered my new purchase under my arm, I left the Town Duck believing a friend in Warrenton might be a possibility.

# Starting to Dance with a Friend

After my first venture, I found myself dropping by the Town Duck to say hello several times a week. I went in to browse the fancy cheeses, the orange and blue pots and pans, and European ceramics. The stimulation to my eyes and appetite enticed me away from Velveeta sandwiches in my mother's brown and cream kitchen with black iron ware and grey metal pots hanging from the walls. Inside the Town Duck, I felt miles and years away from the colorless atmosphere of my troubled past.

And then there was the special energy that Robyn brought to the place; a feeling that kept me looking around, asking questions and making comments with none of the self-consciousness of someone with a socially unacceptable disease. Her extroverted manner encouraged me to stay and chat with her. And when I did, Robyn started to ask me to help with opening boxes, wrapping gifts, and welcoming the new customers into her recently opened shop. Within a month or two, I was almost an employee. The bright and artful windows drew in more and more customers every day.

One day Judy Lieberman stopped in. Judy was a dark- haired dancer from somewhere else. After getting married and moving to one of the first suburbs of Warrenton, Warrenton Lakes, she had started teaching privately in an elementary school off Shirley Highway, Warrenton's in-town bypass. Her specialty was Martha Graham technique, a style of modern dance I had taken in college and in San Francisco. As Robyn and I started talking with her, we quickly realized we shared a love of dance and started attending classes together on a weekly basis.

Dr. Lebensohn was thrilled, of course. Exercise was on his "how to keep Betsy out of the hospital" list. And within a matter of months, I had tackled most of the items. I had learned to drive, bought a car, joined a church, started art class, found a supportive new friend, and now, with my friend, was moving on the dance floor to a beat we both shared.

# Building a Life

B y winter my life was full.

My job was full-time even though as a senior flight attendant I only had to work a few flights a month and only 20 hours a week. My art classes at the Community College and painting in the garage continued. I took walks every day, always stopping by the Town Duck. I went to dance class once a week, attended church several times a month, and took bible study when I could. Daily sitting meditations in front of a candle helped relax me.

Everything but the meditation made me tired. And, along with painting, it was the only non-community- oriented activity that Dr. Lebensohn believed did not put me at risk for another episode.

I was still sick after-all. I was sick because of migraines and recurring sinus infections, because of the way my mind seemed to work... or not work... reminding me there were forces inside my brain that were unpredictable and frightening. When I was on the job flying, I only felt safe limiting my conversations to short, purposeful interaction: "Would you like chicken or beef?" Can I refill your coffee?" The thought that I might enter bizarre behavior if I trespassed into anything more substantial frightened me.

When I talked in art class however, I was much more comfortable. I had opinions I enjoyed sharing with my amiable and open-minded colleagues, many of whom were painting and drawing to help them get beyond a personal obstacle. And with my new friend Robyn, it was easy to talk about anything. She was off beat enough that

I didn't worry about some psychological mishap being taken as strange or off-putting.

But deep inside there was still that nagging feeling that the person others saw in me wasn't there. And sometimes it wasn't. My brother Russell would be talking with me and notice that my eyes would glaze and my body language would show no sign of following our current conversation. I was afraid that others might notice this too. And because I apparently wasn't in control of where my mind went during these times, the "I" that took these far- off journeys seemed separate from the "I" that wanted to feel well and confident.

But this was my state. And Dr. Lebensohn knew all about it. He understood it. He also understood that some aspect of me was real and important. I would share my fears and he would acknowledge them. He would then reassure me that at some point I would be capable, successful, and enjoy my life. He said this with the voice of experience and the heart of respect and compassion. And then, as he looked me straight in the eye, he would say, almost every time we met "Miss Goin, you can only have the life you want if you build it one step at a time." It all made me tired.

# Morning Walks

When you're sick with mental illness, the mentally ill person inside can often feel like your best friend.

Each night after a full day of activities I'd be in bed by 8 o'clock and get up by 7. I'd begin with a long walk by myself, dropping by the pharmacy on Main Street to get a cup of coffee, chatting briefly with those on their way to work in town.

Walking my home- town streets, watching nature and drinking cups of coffee had all been part of my life since my teens. My morning walks were a form of meditation. They were an opportunity to consider what else I needed to do to become more normal as the rhythms of my steps and my observations of the world around me affirmed that I was real. When alone, I felt part of a subtle ecosystem, spiritually joined with the trees and the squirrels. Once faced with having to show people who I was and having to seriously interact with them, the comfort of my surroundings fell apart. I melted into anxiety. Being pulled deeper into wanting to be alone.

For most of my adult life I had rarely taken the time to listen to people. Perhaps because I was overly concerned with protecting myself, keeping my limitations and weaknesses from being discovered during a conversation. I kept my conversations with people short and superficial and would pull away from any sustained subject. It wasn't until much later, after I began getting healthier, that I learned that people, other people, had concerns and problems just like me.

Dr. Lebensohn encouraged my meditation and my walking.

Somehow, as I moved along the streets morning after morning, I began to discover that the world around me was bigger, more interesting, and even safer than the world that existed inside my head.

After years of trying my best to find a path towards normalcy, I had made a small life for myself. I began exploring my interests in the outdoors.

From March through October, I kayaked with my brother and his wife Carol, following her lead like a lemming. I wasn't an accomplished kayaker and had little experience in white water but loved seeing the eagles, deer and beavers along the shore. The combined tranquility and excitement of moving through water captivated me. One minute, I'd be in blissful harmony with the earth, the next, aghast at seeing a large water snake heading for my paddle. When Russell and Carol got divorced, I was on my own but still committed to bonding with nature. Without Carol's help however my experiences turned out unpredictably.

One day in early March I found myself trapped in a fallen tree in the middle of West Virginia assured that the surging current would pull me to the bottom. Not knowing what else to do, I held onto a branch with one hand, my paddle with the other and tried to keep my kayak between me and the water. Within minutes, while calling out for help, it was clear the universe had other plans. The river's force pulled me into its icy waters and held me under the tree while I bobbed for my life. Gratefully, there were others there, more talented than I. They saw my distress, maneuvered their canoes across the current, and positioned themselves to pull me out, conscious, blue as a herring and just barely on the right side of hypothermia. Once dry clothes were found, a fire made, and my kayak retrieved from the rocks below, I had no choice but to reclaim my paddle and push off for the destination. It was good to be alive and good to be floating back home. My death wish had clearly moved on.

As much as I enjoyed water sports, by the next fall my kayak was for sale and my interests had shifted to Astronomy. I had always loved watching the moon and stars whether it was while walking down the streets of Warrenton at night or standing on the Golden Gate Bridge. The enormity of the dark canopy and twinkling jewels dancing in patterns above tree- tops and clouds elevated my senses and stimulated my appreciation for God's handiwork.

I told Dr. Lebensohn what I wanted to do. "What is that Miss Goin?"

"I want to join an astronomy club."

"Well then," he said, "call the Naval Observatory." I did, and they gave me the number for the National Capital Astronomers. Sheer heaven. I finally knew what I wanted to do.

Happily, I drove to The National Capital Astronomers' meetings twenty miles from Warrenton at the Manassas Battlefield Park and admired the mid-night sky through my newly purchased Celestron 8 telescope with the help of a thirteen- year -old sky watcher named Andrew. I learned to both find and identify the constellations that had once seemed so amorphous. I learned to pick out planets and track them, feel the pure joy of meteors flashing brilliantly and then vanishing into the edges of the universe, see Orion patiently hovering overhead allowing me to feel the presence of giants from another time, view Pleiades twinkling in and out of sight assuring me there was hope in the world, and then the reassurance of the Big Dipper looking grand and almost tangible, connecting me to the plight of those who followed the drinking gourd to their freedom in the North. The calmness of watching the galaxy grounded me. Such a different experience from the nights in San Francisco when they zoomed inside my head, pulling me into an outer space that was dark, dangerous and all consuming.

With Dr. Lebensohn's support I sought out what it was that interested me. Because of his encouragement, I wanted to be open to new experiences and activities. At first the challenge was confusing. I was still used to thinking I should do what others did, what was typical among my friends and neighbors. But I wasn't typical and my mental health challenges didn't allow me to be occupied with a family life like others were. But soon I learned to trust my instincts and follow my curiosity in almost anything that came my way except men.

They triggered in me a relic-like response, an old way of feeling about myself as a woman that was confining, hollow, and boring. Dr. Lebensohn hadn't encouraged me either. Instead, he wanted me to focus on grounding my own life. I was grateful for that. But as therapy continued, a time came when he became visibly concerned. My stories all involved too much drinking, an inability to communicate, and strange proposals of marriage and rejections.

Marriage was the furthest thing from my mind. Rather than serving as a social and economic advancement for lowly women, I viewed marriage as a trap, a limitation to a life of independence and adventure.

My experiences, my mental illness and even the distant advice from my own father had caused me to push them into the realm of "the other," to depersonalize them. I now wanted none of it. Doing it all to feel normal, acceptable, just-like-everyone-else felt like being a small wild animal caught in a wire trap. "Men are just toys," I told Dr. Lebensohn. I had no other way to explain it. "Men, marriage, and dating, it's all fake." I could feel my artificial persona buckling inside my head. Something was changing in me as all those confusing memories of men surfaced from my emotional desert. The modern young woman I wanted to be had vacated the premises and I now needed help. I watched as Dr. Lebensohn's fatherly demeanor turned on a dime. "Miss Goin, you cannot hate half the human race." I didn't know why not. He explained it took too much negative energy.

# *Just Say No*

I didn't avoid men. I've always thought good looking men were a joy to behold. But I also knew that they were dangerous. Not by themselves necessarily but in a relationship with me. Their presence and personality knocked me off center; caused me to fall into a hole filled with vague and disturbing memories from my childhood.

And the ghost of my father tainted my choices. I didn't realize that men that drank a lot were risky. I thought most men, like my father and his friends, drank heavily. Binge drinking. My strategy of following what seemed familiar and comfortable caused me to enter into relationships that were unstable and often dangerous.

As I began to get my feet back on the ground with the help of Dr. Lebensohn, it seemed wise and responsible to avoid the challenge of negotiating life with a male partner. In addition to the possibility of a calmer life, the lack of a relationship would prevent having a child. I had been counseled by my doctor not to have any. The fear of the effects of Thalidomide-babies born without arms or legs filled the pages of Life magazine during the 60s, graphically demonstrating how powerful new drugs of the era could reduce discomforts during pregnancy while causing horrible birth defects. Even the medical community was frightened. During one visit to his office, Dr. Lebensohn looked me in the eye as he often did and said, "Miss Goin, you will need to be on drugs the rest of your life and should avoid getting pregnant. How do you feel about that?" I nodded in agreement. I may have even smiled. "Sounds like a good reason to keep my distance from the opposite sex. " It was clear that I was a coward or perhaps beginning to find my way.

# Ups and Downs

S ome people live their lives on a even keel. They come to find that each day is pretty much the same with a few ups and downs and rare opportunities for unpredictable disruptions. I found by my thirties that I was not one of these.

Each day, while working on my recovery, I would wake up unsure as to whether the day would greet me with the makings of a pleasant adventure or result in an emotional helicopter ride. It was Dr. Lebensohn that helped me understand that avoiding digressions into mental illness was my responsibility. He made it clear that a large part of this responsibility included shaping the activities of my waking hours by planning my day, and consistently employing a set of behaviors that would keep me focused and well.

As I struggled to follow Dr. Lebensohn's advice, I would occasionally fall asleep feeling as though the day had been a good one; that I had successfully managed all the do's and don'ts on my list. The attributes were a greater feeling of calm, an ability to trust myself more, an inclination to want to talk more spontaneously because of this sense of trust.

But there was a period when things started to change. During one of my monthly visits, Dr. Lebensohn noticed my symptoms right away. I had lost weight, had dark circles under my eyes, and complained of being tired and afraid. The corners and colors of my world were losing clarity. Paranoia was taking control.

From his distance, Dr. Lebensohn saw all this. He shared with me his concerns and observations. And in his kind fatherly voice, ordered me to take time off from work. "Miss Goin, something is causing you stress. You must relax, rest, and take at least three weeks of medical leave. There isn't an option now."

As he talked with me, I began to realize how warped my thinking was becoming again and I agreed. His intelligence reached out as a lifeline. I began swimming through a sea of perilous thoughts to safer ground. Having discovered this ground during my recovery, I was now able and anxious to separate myself from the delusional thinking and to acknowledge that the other worldly voices calling to me through advertisements and musical lyrics were only a manifestation of my paranoia. From the leather chair in his office, I could now objectify my own illness creeping in through the cracks. I wanted it stopped. Once my 45 minutes of facing reality was up, I walked to my favorite boutique off Connecticut Avenue to chat with my friend Rosemary and browsed the racks. At home the next day, the feeling of relief accompanied my call into work. "Hello, this is Catherine Goin. My doctor says I need time off." The head of the medical department had little to say. He knew my history, flipped through my file, and, finding only notes of good performance, said three weeks would be ok. I agreed to meet with him and Dr. Lebensohn before returning to work.

# Needed Rest

During my three-week absence from work, I rested and took long walks. Dr. Lebensohn had assured me that by monitoring my behavior and taking it easy I could avoid another episode.

Flying was a hard job. Long hours, long periods without food and reliable sleep, adjustments to dramatic time changes, and little time in flight to be by myself. These things, including the strain of needing to be social and always on call, had upset my biorhythms. I learned with Dr. Lebensohn's help that I was prone to upset when tired. Perhaps all of us are but, in my case, a susceptible mind had learned an exit strategy that had proven to be unhealthy and destabilizing.

Looking after myself physically and emotionally was now essential. Because I was clear that I wanted to live an independent life, which included both flying and my long-term mental health, I had to become even more sensitive to things in my life that gave me a sense of structure and peace. Most importantly, I had to avoid over-stimulation. As a single woman without much income, I had found I could easily fill every waking minute with things to do with visiting people, attending lectures and church activities, taking walks, dancing, genealogical clubs, music recitals, and painting. Being spread too thin did more than make me feel stressed and uncomfortable; it caused all the stuff in my life to rattle inside my head, filling me with a sense of imbalance and panic, like I was falling into a pit of snakes.

# The Need for Values

If there's anything comforting about having mental illness, it's that the symptoms can be minimized and even relieved; that life can be lived in an acceptable and mostly enjoyable manner. Getting to this state in my case required the support of Dr. Lebensohn, ongoing medication, a stable job, a mostly quiet living situation, and a realization that I could - and must - manage my health through diet, exercise and minimizing stress. Most importantly for me, it required discovering the need for a set of values.

During my hospitalization and the years following, it became clear that the values my well-intentioned parents might have tried to instill in me had been bent and obscured. When it came to values, the only thing that seemed important was the moment- by- moment thrill of getting away from the mundane and usual. It was all about finding opportunities for adventure and excitement; to push beyond the limitations of the status quo by reading the latest books, going to the opera and ballet at the most exciting venues, traveling to places I'd heard about from The National Geographic, and seeking out associates that would indulge my passion for things like flying in small planes, attending concerts and political demonstrations, going on hiking trips throughout the Rocky Mountains, motorcycling in Hawaii and water skiing.

It was my father who introduced me to water skiing, and I loved it: the speed while soaring across the wakes he'd make with his outboard engine, his encouragement to go faster and faster, the fear of falling into pools of stinging nettles below my skis. That anticipation of almost falling took me to a level unfettered by the social life my mother had hoped for me. My desire to abandon this life was hardly my own making. My brilliant but desperate father who had wanted so much more for himself had surely planted it deep in me as well as my unorthodox brother Russell. Were our lives the embodiment of values he had wanted for himself? Were my passions and aspirations there because he had been the child of a desperately poor farm family from rural Virginia, had been forced to finish his formal education at the end of six grade, had started to work for a living and support himself before the age of sixteen, had missed pursuing a dream of serving in World War II. Somehow, without understanding how any of it had happened, he had become a mismatched husband, a loving but overwhelmed father, and a lonely, tormented man with a drinking problem until his death by suicide in the late 1960s.

Over the years between my first hospitalization and my need to take off from work, I began to envision the possibility that my compulsion to find excitement was somehow associated with my need to escape. I was also beginning to understand that instead of pursuing external stimulation I needed something affirming inside. It was this period that opened a new pathway and helped me realize that my health, my job, my independence, my newfound identity could be lost in an instant and that these things were valuable to me because life was valuable. I was valuable. People and nature were valuable. It was at this point that I realized just going to church as Dr. Lebensohn had encouraged was no longer enough. While I needed a faith tradition to pull me away from my self-absorption and cynicism, I also needed to satisfy something even deeper. With the support of my parish minister, I began to read the Bible to discover the roots of a faith that might help me find a sense of hope that my father or mother had never found.

# Beyond Bible Study

While living with my mother in 1985, I began reading the Bible. The arrangement was a symbiotic one. She provided a roof over my head and a quiet environment. I provided money for her groceries and expenditures and later became her chauffeur.

On Sundays we attended church together. We both dressed up in our best clothes, got into my new AMC car, a brown Spirit, and tried to arrive at church 30 minutes early to get a good parking spot. It never occurred to either of us that my choice of vehicle was an ironic one. The point in driving the short distance was to provide Mama, who was now in her 70s and had become wobbly, and overweight, a safer means of accessing Sunday activities.

Each year, it seemed that Mama's and my interests in church were drawing apart. Mama was a social butterfly with friends she loved gossiping with before and after the service. She especially loved pot- lucks and coffee hours where she talked and nibbled with equal enthusiasm. During the sermons, however, she would excuse herself from all related contemplation, narrow her eyes and sink slowly into the curves of our shared wooden pew.

Although pot- lucks and coffee were essential in getting me to church at the beginning, by the time Mama had started softly snoring through the final hymns, I was drawn to something much deeper. The years of Mama and me attending Bible Study had sparked an interest in understanding the full history and significance of the New and Old Testaments. I was no longer satisfied with the small exposure during weekly services. I wanted to piece together a whole story that made sense to me, that explained why and how the star of the show, Jesus Christ, had become so important to me and others that called themselves Christians.

I began to read the Bible starting with the Gospel of John, the other three Gospels, Psalms, Proverbs, the rest of the New Testament, and finally the Old. It was a self-study program offered by my minister that took a year to complete. I would read on my own, underline sections, place stars by parts I especially liked or didn't understand and, at least once a month, make a visit to the office to discuss my thoughts. A story with characters and colors began to emerge. As I gained insight, the chapters and verses were no longer separate from me but drawn onto a canvas inside my head, at first a series of pictures I could see, then stories I related to, then a connection to a philosophy and set of ideas that helped me recalibrate my values and behaviors. Slowly, through inquiry, I was immersed into what felt like the realm of the sacred.

As I moved through the hundreds of pages reading small sections day after day, I experienced a richness and depth I'd never had before. A confirmed bookworm had discovered the ultimate book with beautiful writing. I was beginning to see the world beyond the confines of a small, sick mind; beyond the myths I had created for myself. It was easy to feel that God was speaking and sharing what He wanted for me. For the first time, I began to experience myself as something more than just a biological being routed in my material surroundings. I began to feel as if part of me was spirit and that this spirit existed in me because of God's presence all around me.

There were many Bible passages that spoke to me. The sounds of the words and rhythms, the use of images; they were written in a way that stirred my heart and inspired me to keep reading and exploring the underlying meaning.

The first one that captured my attention was Psalm 30, verses 11 and 12. It was 1986. Each day I gathered myself into the rocking chair in front of my bedroom window. I placed the open Bible on my lap. The year before I had read the whole Bible, now I was returning to its familiar rooms and passageways, walking around in them again, discovering the deeper colors and tapestries I had missed before.

"You have turned for me my mourning into dancing; you have loosed my sackcloth and clothed me with gladness that my glory may sing your praises and not be silent. Oh Lord My God, I will give thanks to you forever." Ps 30: 11-12 (NKJV)

As I read, bright energy rose from my toes to my spine. Dance had been an important part of my life. There was ballet and tap as a child, modern dance in college, dancing in Hawaii and San Francisco. Now, as an adult in Warrenton, my friend Robyn and I attended a Martha Graham Technique class at the local community center. There I made designs in the air, flew like a bird and sparkled among the clouds. The confines of my short thin body vanished in space as my confidence grew. My doctors had encouraged me to join anything that would stimulate my creativity and sense of self, but little did I realize that this reference to dance and so many other references throughout the Bible would connect me to something beyond the fearful, conflicted life that I wanted to escape. The use of metaphor, of dance as more than dance, of gratitude for life that offered a feeling of going beyond the bounds of a day -to- day life that had previously offered me little. When dancing and while reading the Bible, I was pulled out of my shell and into a realm full of hope and possibilities.

# Discovering Paul

When I first started going to church with my mother, I stepped through the doors easily, figuring all was well. It was when I started paying attention to more than the pleasant words and enchanting rhythms of Sunday services that I realized that vulnerability not happiness was the first call to a life of meaning and faith.

It was when I started working through the words of Saint Paul that I was forced to face up to the person I had become and likely had always been; someone who, as a young and adventurous child of the 60s, had acted in ways that were obsessed with the aggrandizement of self, not in a mean or power- hungry way but out of the small and desperate need to become less of the person that felt fearful and threatened by powers I didn't think I had or understood.

Prior to his conversion from Judaism, Paul had been a persecutor of Christians as Nero, the Emperor of Rome, was. But during a trip to Syrian Damascus, Paul had a stunning experience. A bright light and a mysterious voice came to him and called him on his hatred of Jesus, who he considered a blasphemous rabble-rouser. For three days Paul was blinded, then, with the help of a Christian named Ananias, his sight returned. His life changed radically. Instead of returning to a life as a hater of Christians, he became a fervent apostle of Jesus and a fatherly figure to young men like Timothy.

One of the two letters Paul wrote to Timothy was written while he was in prison. He was there, wrongly charged along with other

Christians, for setting fire to the Roman capital and sentenced to death by Nero.

When I first read Paul's letters, I found his tone and ideas abrasive. I found his message restrictive and antithetical to my belief in the importance of independence and choice in life.

In Paul's world, as a conservative Jew, women had no role as leaders or independent adults. Homosexuals, adulterers, non-married men and women were explicitly condemned for their sexual practices. In his letters, Paul decries these acts as sinful but, rather than condemning these acts in accordance with the law, Paul believed acceptance of oneself, and others was essential. Loving oneself and one's neighbor were not contradictory but a source of authentic and balanced power.

While trying to relate to what I was reading, I began to feel a need to contemplate my life. Was it possible that my self-centered, partying lifestyle qualified as sinning? Were my bad life choices as a young adult responsible for accentuating the lack of self-worth and balance in my life? Was my feeling of dis-ease that had deepened into a schizophrenic episode been planted inside my head by my sense of alienation from my troubled father and mother? And had they, like me, been unable to find the peace and personal acceptance that God wanted for all of us? Were these our problems? While trying to understand Paul, I felt uncomfortable and lonely. I wondered how I might get out of the bind my past or blindness had set for me.

I took my time with Paul, working through his language, attending Bible studies, reading books, watching old Bible movies, all trying to understand where Paul was coming from, why he was such an important figure in the early Christian Church.

Slowly I began to realize Paul's choices, like mine, had brought him pain and alienation. He had created a life colored by mistrust, an eye for an eye mentality, and the need to rise above and defeat those with ideas that threatened his ideology. I began to see that Paul had to work at learning how to love. He had to learn how to transform a life rooted in the Old Testament and to begin to love himself and others as exemplified by Jesus Christ.

I discovered that it was Paul's role to help us understand that, despite one's past and point of view, one could find a life of meaning through a willingness to be vulnerable and open; to move beyond one's blindness and see the world more holistically. As I began to work and stumble through these ideas, one day the following passage hit me like a ton of bricks:

"God has not given us a spirit of fear, but of power and of love and of a sound mind." 2 Timothy: 1: 7 (NKJV)

# A Sound Mind

A sound mind. I couldn't imagine anything more important and illusive. At the time, everyone seemed so clear-headed compared to me. And yet, according to Paul, a sound mind was available to me and others like me who were confused, lonely, and alienated from a sense of self.

According to Paul, a sound mind wasn't an accident, it was a gift; one that could pull us away from fear; one that in conjunction with love and compassion, could transform us from an unhealthy state into a state of peace, clarity and purpose.

Those words from Paul gave me a hint at clarity and courage: clarity to see that there was something beyond the symptom of isolation that my disease had instilled in me, and courage to try to absolve it; to experiment with behaviors that felt alien to the frozen buried self that I'd been harboring inside for years.

For years, holding a conversation had been purely utilitarian. I talked when I had to talk; when I needed something; if the topic was art, especially when it involved me and art. I rarely initiated any exchange with people who I didn't know. Feelings of inferiority kept me focused on me and ways to protect myself from others finding out how dead I was.

But Paul inspired me. He was highly educated, and he had transformed the way he looked at himself: from a respected persecutor of Christians to a sinner of the first order, and finally to a beloved child of God despite his prior actions. He was a bulldog:

a former Pharisee who had made his peers angry to the point of wanting to kill him, yet he continued along a path he knew in his heart was right and true. He also had a message to share with others that helped them see life in a more beautiful way even during times of widespread persecution and fear.

I discovered through Paul that people who have a noble mission, one they believe in and that helps others, and they pursue this mission amidst difficulties and dangers; these kinds of people can lift us out of our discomforts, our pain, and our illusion that life has no meaning or purpose other than the material.

If having a sound mind was a gift from God and if God was real, then I too must have one. And if I had one, maybe I needed to consciously work at activating it by living a life focused on some purpose and meaning that was beyond the limitation of an illusionary self, a self I had built out of fear, loss and a lack of connectivity to others. A life alone was antithetical to Paul's life and message. Instead of maintaining my thinly constructed veneer and maintaining my distance and isolation, it occurred to me I needed to reach out and begin to take new risks.

Having a sound mind was about being able to focus on what was important and true. This is when Dr. Lebensohn told me "Miss Goin, I admire your steely determination." I was floored.

"Finally, brethren, whatever things are true, whatever things are noble, whatever things are just, whatever things are pure, whatever things are lovely, whatever things are of good report, if there is any virtue, and if there is anything praise-worthy, meditate on these things." Philippians 4:8 (NKJV)

# *Conversations*

E ven before I became inspired by Paul's message, Dr. Lebensohn insisted that I participate in conversations.

"You can't be so involved in yourself," he would say. "You must reach out to others. Only then will you discover that people are approachable, interesting and have problems as you do; that you are connected to them."

Every day he required I talk with people. I did as I was told. Despite my feelings of inferiority and self-doubt, I forced myself to strike up conversations with passengers on my flights or those I would run into along the streets of Warrenton.

Dr. Lebensohn was the wise, self-aware parent I never had. His position of authority and professionalism compelled me to direct my attention away from the attractiveness of my disease and towards a life outside myself even though it was more difficult and scarier. His clarity and kindness inspired me to seek out others rather than retreat into my self-absorption.

Paul's message was also clear. It flowed from a story of personal pain and difficulty to which I could relate. His writings conveyed a wise and persevering man of God who had discovered himself after leaving a corrupted life. He had redeemed himself by shedding a life of intolerance and persecution. Yet, how was it possible that someone so reprehensible could transform themselves? How was it possible that someone as clearly sinful as a Pharisee could, as a new Christian, come to so easily criticize the sinning of others?

Initially upon reading I found his unequivocal message offensive, morally conservative, and alien to my modern lifestyle. His use of words, however, his images and the logical pattern of his thoughts inspired me to look beneath my first impressions. I kept reading, kept studying, experimented with my own interactions with people and ideas. Finally, something broke for me. Paul's words began to feel familiar and comforting. They aroused in me a willingness to question my own viewpoint and lifestyle. I began to imagine a transformation. Rather than letting myself remain stuck in ways that no longer served me, I found an opening to something more compelling and inspiring. I found, through Paul, the capacity within myself to transform an abstract God into a powerful and loving presence.

# *The Day I Met Maya Anjelou*

A conversation with Maya Anjelou was one of three conversations that helped open my eyes.

It was a flight from Dulles to San Francisco. She was sitting in first class, seat 7B, back near the galley of the stretch DC 8, and I was working as "galley slave" preparing food and carts for dinner service.

After dinner was over and the movie was being shown, somehow Maya and I started talking. The movie didn't interest her and without warning, this kind-faced African American women called out to me, "You've been busy this evening." Her powerful voice had a resonance I'd not experienced. But I was exhausted with no sleep from the night before and feeling stressed by all the responsibilities: getting the food warmed, organizing the china and glassware, mixing drinks, asking for dinner selections, and trying not to appear uncool, distracted, and mentally unfit for my job. But this woman with the interesting voice wanted to talk and because I couldn't be rude or unprofessional, we slowly began an exchange that continued for almost an hour.

What I remember was her ability to turn our time together into a most satisfying exchange. I found myself sharing my story while encouraging her to do the same. There was a need on my part to understand who she was. Her face and animation fascinated me; her ideas about writing and art, her experiences with trauma, her period of withdrawal as a child. She told me there was a time she chose not to talk, a time when fear trapped her inside herself. By asking questions, by telling me things I somehow needed to know, I felt connected to her and at ease in a way I hadn't remembered.

With her, I shared my love of painting and dance, my bout with mental illness and anorexia, my love of flying. As she listened, her words of encouragement cheered me on. Yet I didn't really know her, of course. I didn't even know her name, and her reputation was not familiar to me. What I did know was that she was accomplished, grounded and remarkably sane. Her grace and presence were palpable even to a tired, self-absorbed flight attendant who, moments before, had been on the edge of crying. Whoever she was, she transported me to another state of being and inspired possibility.

As our conversation began to close, she mentioned having written a book and encouraged me to read it. She said she wrote it to make sense out of senselessness. She wanted it to be read as a way of reaching out to others and of showing that a life full of lemons can be made into lemonade. On my layover in San Francisco, I went directly to the bookstore. Her book was waiting for me on the shelf: "I Know Why the Caged Bird Sings."

# Meeting Ansel Adams

On a spring morning heading for San Francisco from Dulles Airport I learned that a Mr. Adams was one of the few first-class passengers. His name, "Ansel Adams," was on the manifest and he sat alone at the lounge table. I had admired him and his work since college art classes at William and Mary. His photography of natural places was world famous… his pictures of mountains, rivers, and sky graced calendars, coffee table books, museums and art galleries. And now here he was, a few feet away from me as I attended to my galley duties, setting up carts and trays, preparing meals so I could avoid traveling down the aisles and interacting with people.

But I had to talk to him. My fear of conversation hid beneath my need to reach out to the lifeline his beautiful photographs had offered me and my generation, to share with him my love of the soulfulness he'd found within the black and white ripples of stone and water, to let him know of how his work had inspired my brother to find nobility in the faces of war-tired peasants in Vietnam through his Japanese camera. Somehow, his presence represented a monumental hallowedness that allowed the dark struggle of Vietnam, the grand beauty of the earth, my own struggle and deep appreciation for art and artists to merge into one.

"So nice to see you Mr. Adams. I'm a fan of yours and a low-level painter who'd like to get better. Any suggestions?" My boldness startled me, but I couldn't retreat. He looked up, smiled, and asked if I might sit with him. I remember thinking he's like Dr. Lebensohn:

dignified, old fashioned, someone who knows how to make people feel comfortable. I accepted his invitation, and a conversation began. He told me he loved to fly, loved to look out over the earth below and to take in the forms and shadows. He mentioned paintings by Georgia O'Keefe he admired with clouds and blue sky, the artist looking down from a plane. I told him I'd seen one like that and loved it as well.

We moved to the large window across the aisle, and he talked more about how he saw landscapes. He asked me about my paintings and what I enjoyed looking at. I told him I loved bold colors, tended to work in two dimensions, and mostly painted people. He listened, asked questions, and shared with me the necessity of concentration, of seeking out the beauty in things no matter what, of being humble and focused on the presence of places and people, large and small.

It was time to return to my duties and the next service. I thanked him for his good advice and, with difficulty, moved back to the galley. I had been touched by a great genius I thought, one that balanced wisdom with hard work, hard work with a joy of living, a kind heart with a love of truth. So few moments yet their largeness was inescapable.

# Meeting Deepak Chopra

My meeting with Ansel Adams took place sometime in the late 1980s. During this period and into the 90s I began to follow Dr. Lebensohn's advice to try different forms of meditation as means of better focusing my mind.

When I was sick, my thinking and emotions ricocheted from one thing to another; each thought and idea, disconnected from the next. There was no ability to distract the almost constant flurry. And while the meditation softened it and made it feel less invasive, there was no coherency and no ability to experience anything but the ongoing roar of multiple inner engines exploding in different directions. When working as a flight attendant, I attempted to manage the excess cylinders as an overwhelmed fire fighter, trying to divert the next explosion, trying to contain the flashes inside my head that I'd learned were not normal or healthy. As a control strategy, I worked hard at engaging with people during work and social events. I wanted to gain confidence this way, yet I was forced to spend time alone, trying to keep my mind quiet, grounded and somewhat orderly. I had learned the hard way that over-stimulation was dangerous, that my overstimulated mind was especially dangerous if I let it willfully wrap around bad thinking and compulsions.

When my minister invited me to attend contemplative prayer sessions, it seemed like an opportunity to work on myself. Once a week, I'd arrive at the church's Ladies Lounge to join others in first listening to a religious reading by Thomas Merton and then spending 20 minutes meditating on it. Somehow the rhythm and accessibility of the language spoke to me. Instead of adding more data and stimulation to my raging mind, it provided a quality, almost like music, to a place deep and uncontaminated. After several months of these sessions, I was finding confidence in their being a part of me that had survived my mental illness.

This was my first introduction to group meditation, and it proved refreshing and helpful. Reflecting on the power and nature of God after an adult discussion was much more complete and satisfying than sitting alone in my studio staring at a candle, feeling lonely, and hoping to find enlightenment. I continued with this group for almost a year. On my own, I used it to uncover the hidden nuances of Bible passages as well as generating a reliable alternative to my negative thinking. Meditation allowed me to feel quiet, present and whole and to disengage from the compulsion to explode in all directions. It enabled my chemistry to finally make peace with itself.

On the day I met Deepak Chopra, the topic of meditation captivated our exchange. Mr. and Mrs. Chopra were first class passengers on a 767 from Heathrow, London to Dulles and then on to San Francisco.

I'd never heard of Mr. Chopra, didn't know of his fame or his background in medicine and spirituality, but somehow none of this mattered. While I was sitting on my jump seat, he stopped to talk, complementing the mixed grill he'd had for dinner and sharing his purpose for travel. I saw at once that he twinkled. His sense of fun and intelligence came together in a flash. Within a few minutes, I was inviting him to sit next to me and began asking him questions as I noticed his vegetarian wife sleeping in her seat twelve feet or so away.

He talked easily with a slight accent that required I concentrate. He spoke of his work writing, lecturing, counseling others in living mindfully. His work was obviously his passion, and I was struck by his devotion to helping others.

I shared with him my experience with meditation, and he was

excited about how I thought it benefited me. He mentioned he'd recently written two books, "Ageless Body, Timeless Mind" and "The Seven Spiritual Laws of Success" both of which explored the relationship between what and how we think and who we become. His insights intrigued me and made me want to learn more but it was time to get back to work. As he returned to his still sleeping wife, I busied myself with tea service.

Several weeks after our conversation, "The Seven Spiritual Laws of Success by Deepak Chopra arrived at my mother's house, its pages filled with advice that resonated with me. I felt honored that Dr. Chopra had remembered me with such a gift. And then, as I turned the pages of the book, I noticed the name of one of the chapters: The Law of Giving. As I read through it, I could feel his energy inspiring my own.

According to Dr. Chopra, the Universe operates through dynamic exchanges. By giving, one can participate.

I had experienced the "dynamics of the Universe" when severely disturbed prior to my hospitalization. But this was a form of energy that swirled me into isolation and disassociation; that occupied my time and drained me of any ability to focus on useful things. Dynamic exchange as suggested in this book was the direct opposite. Giving, as a manifestation of this dynamic exchange, creates energy that then turns into more energy. I decided to try giving away things beginning with my paintings. The rational was promising. I wanted my paintings of abstract, brightly colored people, cats and plants to have a happy home away from the dark basement where they'd been gathering dust and mold and taking up space. Russell (I was living with my brother at this time) needed for his mechanical treasures. As I started to give them away, I began having exchanges that were joyful. I'd offer a friend a painting, they would smile and look amused and then we'd talk about what they liked or didn't like about it in a free- spirited kind of way. I also began giving complements to friends and strangers. While waiting in line at the Safeway, I would see a woman in an unusual color that looked striking on her and would point that out trying to hold a smile on my face to make sure she didn't miss the point of my observation. In return, the warmth, the smile, the energy from the comment would be extended back to me. A conversation would arise that was pleasant and often filled with a personal story or a wholesome reflection on life. And these exchanges created a multiplication effect. I'd give a painting or a brief complement and that gave me a sense of powerfulness, not as an individual but as part of a source of power that flowed through everything. In response to this law of giving, I decided that giving gifts, even mental gifts of recognition and silent acknowledgement, should be part of my everyday experience, and learning how to gratefully accept gifts from others was put on my to-do list.

In reflecting on my conversations with Ansel Adams and Maya Angelou, I realized that in these cases as well the messages were all about giving graciously. In the case of Maya, she so graciously gave me her time, her experiences and insight that encouraged me to start talking with people, start to break out of my shell because in doing so I might tap into a source of energy that was freeing and hope filled. In the case of Ansel Adams, he gave me a sense of his passion to art and nature that he was only able to actualize because of a willingness to focus and persevere regardless of the difficulties of one's circumstances. He listened to me graciously without showing any indication that I was less than worthy of his full respect and powerful attention.

# Life in the 90s

I kept flying throughout the 90s and continued following Dr. Lebensohn's advice for good living and reflected on my privileged conversations I had had above the clouds.

Because of my seniority at United, I had plenty of time to pursue things that interested me - everything except cooking, a realm that belonged solely to my mother. I painted often, continuing to give away many of the canvases, started taking flute lessons at the home of a local resident, began creative writing classes at the community college, drove mother on visits and errands, and attended church and meditated on my own. My dance card was full and demanding even as my mental confusion had mostly dissipated. Things seemed promising.

My years of therapy and medication were finally paying off. The ongoing meetings with Dr. Lebensohn, his prescription of a single medication that kept away the voices and the desire to harm myself and with my own emerging desire to stay alive allowed me to move from the need to keep busy throughout the day to a long-term process of figuring out how I might live a life worth living even if short. One of the challenges was accepting the miserable side effects. Among other things, the daily prescription caused problems with balance, a dry mouth that kept me awake long hours at night, and sun sensitivity. I coped by walking and driving carefully, taking naps during the day, and wearing hats and long sleeves. I pretended these were normal considerations for someone who would likely die before age 66. My thinking was still compulsive, often occupied with ideas that had come from the wild blue sky.

In truth, however, people I knew in the 90s were dying. Strokes, heart disease, horrible cancers, and disabling diabetes seemed everywhere: among my friends and family, in my local peer group around town, and even with those much younger. Although my mother was in her eighties and active, the longevity for schizophrenics was far less than the norm. I was willing to face the fact that I might not be around very long. But one year turned into the next and, remarkably, I found myself caught up in adventures and pursuits that challenged my brain and helped me puzzle together a sense of purpose over the years.

I began writing a book, volunteered to assist the troops of Desert Storm and Desert Shield, traveled to Peru to learn about Inca history and spirituality, embarked on a missionary trip to Haiti just before and during the earthquake, and was baptized in the Jordan River in Israel. My chance baptism was the highlight of my life…December 19, 1999.

In 1998, Dr. Lebensohn retired from his practice at age 89. I was devastated but quickly moved on to another doctor he had waiting in the wings, Dr. Goldstein.

In 2001, my flight was stranded in Germany during the immediate aftermath of September 11th. Over a seven- day period, I watched myself maintaining a degree of calm as people in the airport, the hotel and along the streets of Frankfurt responded erratically to fear and loss of control. I remember thinking how strange it seemed that I was mentally fine - processing the situation, accepting that being in control wasn't in my or anyone's ballpark at this time. Ironically, I thought, masses of sane people all around me were medicating themselves with alcohol because the world as they had known it seemed to be turning upside down. By this time in my life, my resources, inside and out, were able to keep my upside- down tendencies nicely right- side up. While I was physically stranded and forced to figure out how to spend my no-flight days positively occupied, my sense of adventure and my ability to now connect to people prevailed without panic or despair. The weather was lovely, an international cinema across the river provided entertainment, and the hotel, trying to accommodate a small portion of the thousands of people not able to travel by air, provided food and lodging with the hospitality of a more well-mannered era.

In 2003, I retired from United, worn out from long trips and no longer inspired by speed and new first- class attitudes. After September 11 the airline industry had changed. Regimentation, suspicion and shabby service had replaced the remnants of an industry that had once advertised their brand with words like friendly, courteous, comfortable and relaxing.

At the age of 90, my mother was forced to move to a local nursing home. Falls, degenerative diseases and a compendium of drugs hit her hard over a period of a few years. Because both of my doctors encouraged me to continue to live with another person - to help ground me and keep me in touch with reality - I moved in with my brother Russell. My mother's house, the house of my youth, was now falling apart and would have been declared uninhabitable by the authorities.

# *Mama Dies*

The process of Mama moving into the nursing home happened quickly. One night she fell from a chair while watching television. Working together, Russell and I got her into her bed. Later that night, after Russell had returned to his house, she fell again, this time in her bathroom. On the brown linoleum floor, her 180 pounds laid unresponsive, her speech hard to understand. Within minutes, the ambulance arrived from the local fire department and three large men maneuvered her body into a large stretcher, down the narrow staircase, and out the front door to the Emergency Room. There was no medical explanation for Mama's rapid downward turn. Within a few hours, she was admitted to the hospital on the hill and within a week transferred to the nearby nursing home unable to care for herself, unable to talk without slurring her words, and now turning visits from her two children into tortuous commentary about how neglectful and selfish we were. Despite our attempts at making something better, week after week consisted of Mama lying in bed, playing bingo and cards and using a wheelchair to find a sense of freedom she'd never known.

After cleaning out her house, Russell and I sold it by auction. With the proceeds, we paid for her care over a seven- year period. When the money was gone, the only recourse was Medicaid. Our combined retirement amounted to less than the monthly nursing home costs and Russell's cottage of a house with small doors, two tiny upstairs bedrooms with a single bath provided no suitable space for Mama and her wheelchair.

Every day, I'd take a trip to visit Mama and, in the spirit of the fifth commandment I attempted to assist her with whatever care I could. For all she had done for me, I wanted to honor her. But with her declining health and the physical distance between us now, the state of our relationship morphed into a place of unhappiness.

Mama's behavior spilled from a place I tried to understand. Was it her marriage? The drinking? The loneliness? Had her family before Russell and me whittled away her sense of self and purpose? Would she have been happier without children and a home that occupied and likely limited her? In the nursing home, I watched Mama as she put aside a mask of a better nature: the mother who cooked and cared for me when I was sick, who tried to maintain a quality of life at which she failed, who lived through the suicide of a husband who she loved despite his demons, who she fought with and watched drink himself to death. And while Mama was smart and outgoing, the move to the nursing home accelerated a downward trend towards darkness and despair. Each time we'd visit, she'd complain about patients and staff stealing from her and tell us, in a voice that was almost inaudible, that we'd made her whole life miserable.

Mama's anger at me and Russell was surprising I thought. Perhaps it was dementia, perhaps the collection of high-level drugs with powerful side effects, or maybe the ghosts she could no longer hold back any longer. When we visited, her skills at hitting below the belt and sinking in her nails were remarkable. It felt like we were the remaining enemies she had to attack in order to save herself. I would have never imagined her that way.

Yet, as she declined, I began to understand that something in our relationship had always been disturbing. The world in which she was rooted nourished behaviors and attitudes that had unsettled something deep inside me. I'd experienced their subtle presence throughout my childhood. Now, with them more fully revealed and as a recovering and more aware adult, I could see them for what they were and found the pain and confusion a disturbing remnant of my childhood's desire to escape into places far away. Dr. Goldstein was concerned that the effect of my mother's regression might trigger regression in me. At his request, I limited my visits to once a week accompanied by Russell or a supportive friend. The sharp words and biting humor continued. Yet never, until the very end, did she stop playing the role of the social butterfly, rolling down hallways in carefully selected outfits, charming her nursing home friends and caretakers with gossip and stories, and showing the world around her that her family's credentials were far above average. Her last words to us were "Leave me now, I'm going to sleep." She died just before her 99th birthday.

# *Home*

In 2006, I moved less than a block away to Russell's. I would have a bedroom, a place for a computer and my books. I'd also have somewhere to store my paintings, china, glassware and the cooking instruments I'd accumulated over the past thirty years.

Despite all the paraphernalia, I'd never cooked and never learned how to cook. Mama had always prepared the meals when I lived at home and, when I lived on my own, I'd always eaten out except for staples like yogurt, fruit, and salads. I was a whiz at assemblage and found I could buy, coordinate and eat non-cooked, mostly vegetarian foods with little regret or expense. Staying away from meal preparation was part of my anorexic eating disorder. It also kept me employed as one of the stewardess-slim women of the friendly skies and helped me fantasize myself as a glamorous super model, a little like Twiggy I wished. I collected kitchenware not for cooking, but because the colorful dishes, pots and pans behind cabinets in my 17 apartments over a ten -year period somehow grounded me. Perhaps they represented the potential I might someday have for competence around making a home even when my career and lack of mental health pulled me away from any home I'd ever had or hoped to have.

At Russell's I finally had a home, not a house but a place to experiment with food and try my hand at entertainment. No longer having to care for Mama, I had time now to prepare whole meals for myself as well as enjoy the creativity of hosting others for dinner and food related celebrations. I'd always enjoyed serving meals to passengers. Now with the transition to Russell's, I began associating food with enjoyment. Dr. Lebensohn had died by now but his encouragement to reach out and be creative inspired me to view food as an extension of his counsel instead of the potential for weight gain and dieting. With the help of my friend Robyn and others, my dishes, pots and pans were no longer a symbol of a life I had always hoped for but one of the resources I now had for nourishing all aspects of my new life.

In addition to learning to cook, I now also had time and space to learn to play guitar. It was Christmas. I wondered into Warrenton's only music store, Drum and Strum, and there on the wall was a beautiful acoustic guitar, the first guitar I'd held since having a small Gibson stolen from my dorm room in college. Buying it, taking lessons, learning to play the blues, learning to play with others; I was beginning to feel at home in a welcoming universe.

# *Psychotherapy*

"Miss Goin, how are you doing today?"

I'd been seeing Dr. Lebensohn for 25 years when he announced his retirement. During the appointment, it was strange there was no Dr. Lebensohn, no father figure, only a greeting I had heard hundreds of times before. Yet this doctor was 35 years younger than Dr. Lebensohn, small like Dr. Lebensohn, articulate, and enormously kind and attentive. Dr. Lebensohn had made sure that before he became unavailable, a suitable doctor would take his place. Dr. Goldstein was affiliated with Georgetown University with a specialty in bi-polar disorder and had an office in the same brick building I'd visited right after my release from the hospital. Now, 25 years later, I was suspicious and worried. Despite that, I knew the doctor that had held me by the hand for so many years had to be trusted to find me an appropriate replacement. Who else would take me on? Who else would be primed to know all I'd been through without having me relive my past? And, without a doctor, I would be lost and isolated. I had no choice but to say goodbye to my beloved mentor and pray that his love and guidance would continue despite my uncertainty.

My first visit with Dr. Goldstein was a reminder that good doctors are benevolent strangers. His manner was quiet but direct. His gaze was relaxed but attentive. Over the period of the first 45 minutes, I told him of how I had lied to Dr. Lebensohn only once but realized Dr. Lebensohn knew; of how I enjoyed being a

Christian and believing God had intervened on my behalf; how I was accustomed to using meditation, yoga and walking to help me feel calmer. He noticed I was overweight and suggested I lose somepounds. I agreed. He referenced the medication I was on and said even though it was an older drug he'd like to keep me on it since it was working well. I said I was glad. We talked about my interest in painting and playing the flute, my challenging living arrangement with my mother, my job as a flight attendant and why I loved it. While Dr. Lebensohn would have asked question after question to get me to speak up, with Dr. Goldstein things were different. I was talking more, initiating more information. After twenty- five years, I had finally lost the fear of sharing myself through conversation. Instead of feeling inferior and unworthy, I found myself in the moment, blabbing on and on with someone I wanted to get to know and to hear him say, "You're doing very well Miss Goin."

As we got to know each other over the first year, I discovered that while Dr. Lebensohn never encouraged me to talk about my past, Dr. Goldstein did. It never felt invasive. He never brought it up. But if I mentioned my parents, my childhood or was bothered about something, he'd subtly introduce a line of commentary that would invite me to go deeper into my own thinking and sometimes into my past. I would add word after word, turning thoughts that barely entered my awareness into statements that felt natural and freeing. I often didn't know where they'd come from or realize they'd been long locked inside my pre- frontal cortex.

One day I mentioned something I'd never brought up in therapy before: my father's suicide. It had been a part of me since the day it happened in the mid-60s when he was 57 and I was 26 living in Alexandria. Mama called me early in the morning. I was headed out the door to work. "I have bad news for you," she said. "Your father killed himself." Her voice, like the sound of a mallet beating on a wooden barrel, was cold and hollow. She went on, blow by blow, as to what had happened. The pictures with sounds and then abrupt silence flashed in front of me. I watched my beloved, angry, desperate father lose his mind in Technicolor. I felt the weight and power of it slam into my chest, breaking and draining me onto my kitchen floor.

A call to the United crew desk came next. "But you can't take sick leave at the last minute." I did of course and within hours Russell arrived at my apartment in Alexandria to pick me up. Within days, there was a funeral. I wore a navy- blue dress and a matching hat. My father's dog, Oscar, the ancient dachshund, had gone mad the night of my father's death, howling and running into walls and furniture. The best solution was to put him to sleep, to let him be company for my father's departure into smoke and ashes.

Sharing my father's death with Dr. Goldstein provided a purging for me. The time was right. Enough distance and experiences had blunted the worst of the trauma. Now, sharing the story of who my father was, how he'd grown up, what he'd been through and to what he'd been subjected provided feelings of both pride and sorrow. In addition to a surplus of alcohol and mental health challenges, the agricultural poisons he'd used for work had taken their toll in the form of early signs of cancer. "Your father didn't stand a chance," Dr. Goldstein said. I had never thought of it that way, but it now made sense. A good, smart, well- intentioned man who had all the grit in the world but none of the education, resources or appropriate care had been dealt a life that he was not equipped to handle. And yet my father had stood up for me, cared about me, encouraged me to study music and art, to attend a good college, to establish a career and independence, to avoid the loneliness and pain he had suffered because he didn't know another way.

After talking about my father, neither of us brought the subject up again for many years. There were other things that seemed more significant as I continued to adjust to the process of keeping grounded and well.

After my first few months of seeing Dr. Goldstein, I joined Weight Watchers. Becoming a member of a group to help me find a more appropriate weight seemed like a step in the right direction. The encouragement of others and the awards built into the program enabled me to lose 26 pounds in a year. Eating less and exercising more nourished my self-esteem and demonstrated that food was not the enemy as I had believed for years.

In addition to encouraging me to lose weight, Dr. Goldstein also requested that I take nutritional supplements. His rationale was that the stress I'd experienced would be taking its toll. He didn't recommend a particular make or brand and admitted knowing little about nutrition. What he did know was that without good physical health, my mental health would take a spiral downward and I needed to attend to both. With the help of my friend Robyn, I found a company, USANA Health Sciences established by Dr. Myron Wentz, that offered a range of products focused on preventing chronic degenerative diseases. Dr. Gold stein, along with the experience of my mother's decline, turned me into a health nut.

From 1998 to the present, I still meet with Dr. Goldstein every three months. At the beginning of each session, he asks me "Miss Goin, how are you doing today? Without hesitation I spew out a series of tidbits, small, insignificant and benevolent pieces that silently and calmly flow together into a whole and complete life. Nothing big, nothing notable but it all comes together like an amazing, wondrous puzzle, a miracle from God for which I'll be forever grateful.

The end!

PS---I forgot to mention how very important the place of music plays in my life and in my recovery. Today I still can't sing but am learning to play the flute, the mandolin and the guitar. Listening to the music of others is of paramount importance…both now and in the past.

Printed in the United States
by Baker & Taylor Publisher Services